To nan and Grandad

From your little poem Writer

love chris xxxxxxxxx

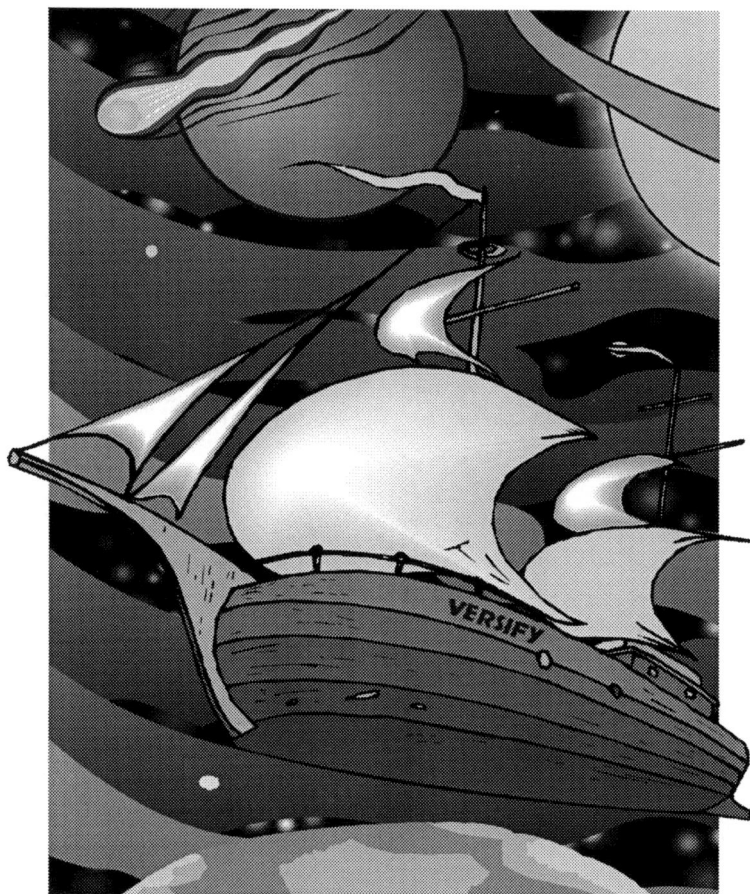

POETIC VOYAGES
SOUTH HAMPSHIRE

Edited by Lucy Jeacock

First published in Great Britain in 2002 by
YOUNG WRITERS
Remus House,
Coltsfoot Drive,
Peterborough, PE2 9JX
Telephone (01733) 890066

HB ISBN 0 75433 484 8
SB ISBN 0 75433 485 6

FOREWORD

Young Writers was established in 1991 with the aim to promote creative writing in children, to make reading and writing poetry fun.

This year once again, proved to be a tremendous success with over 88,000 entries received nationwide.

The Poetic Voyages competition has shown us the high standard of work and effort that children are capable of today. It is a reflection of the teaching skills in schools, the enthusiasm and creativity they have injected into their pupils shines clearly within this anthology.

The task of selecting poems was therefore a difficult one but nevertheless, an enjoyable experience. We hope you are as pleased with the final selection in *Poetic Voyages South Hampshire* as we are.

CONTENTS

Declan Johnson	76

North Baddesley County Junior School

Lisa Hancock	77
Lewis Down	78
David Clamp	78
James Bullock	79
David Goodwin	80

Rookesbury Park School

Chelsea Hayward	80
Hannah Furby	81
Allix Moore	81
Fiona Findlater	82
Jasmine Riggs-Bristow	82
Victoria Mathias-Jones	83
Sarah-Lucille Forfar	83
Daisy White	84
Sophie White	84
Bryony Hayward	85
Lauren Davis	85
Fiona Fairbairn	86
Nicola Cartwright	86
Clementine Turner-Powell	87
Harriet Dunkason	87
Katie Blunden	88
Svetlana Kotova	88
Stephanie Melvin	89
Majiri Otobo	90
Antonia Sugden	90
Elena Preston-Davis	91
Camilla Culshaw	91
Stephanie Dampney	92
Sophie Brown	92
Laura Parker	93
Gilly Windebank	93
Olivia Galloway	94
Elo Otobo	94

Lauren Burton	95
Laura Wagstaff	95
Charlotte Boardman	96
Laetitia Clarke	96
Tilly Wheating	97
Tara Wheating	97
Alice Pollock	98
Queenie Lin Qing Qing	99
Caroline Butten	99
Aleshia Fung	100
Charlotte Gill	100
Hannah Whittle	101

St Mary's RC Primary School, Gosport

Sophie Bourke	101
Chelsea Ferrol	102
Sarah Kelly	102
Skye Hall	103
Rachel Landon	104
Jane Swords	105
Kathleen Smith	106
Samantha Fairclough	106

St Patrick's Catholic Primary School, Woolston

Jacob Wilson	107
Kirsty Lee	107
Cameron Hall	108
Amy Stokes	108
Christopher Lee	108
Caroline Misselbrook	109
Ellen Mooney	109
Jeanne-Irène Zimmermann	110
Leo Jack	110
Yasmin Kitchen	111
Emily Whitmarsh	111
Connor Barnett	112
Chelsea Helliwell	112
Joe Cameron	113

Upham CE Primary School

The Poems

SUMMERTIME BY THE POOL

Sitting by the poolside,
Under my umbrella,
Melting ice cream in my hand,
More sun than anywhere else,
Exciting on the beach,
Relaxing all day long,
Time is going faster,
Interesting shells,
Meeting loads of friends,
Extremely hot,
Beach ball in the pool,
Yachts sailing in the sea,
They're speeding along.

Hannah Robson (9)
Alverstoke CE Junior School

ME IN THE SUMMER

In the summer I like to play,
I like to splash
In the warm relaxing pool.
I get out of the pool,
I go and fill the jug with ice and water,
Then I go and get an ice cream,
I get my yellow sunglasses and sunbathe,
I get back in the blue water,
Mum calls me for an ice cream,
But she forgets about the ice cream,
She says, 'What has happened to your back?'

Sam Evans (10)
Alverstoke CE Junior School

A SUMMER'S DAY

A hot summer's day by the beach,
A light breeze,
What can I hear?
The sea crashing over the rocks,
Crashing, crashing,
My shoulders are scorched,
The birds are singing out loud,
Tweet, tweet.
I am going into the sea,
I am cooling down,
Go back to the sandy beach
To sunbathe.
What can I see?
Children playing.
It is getting hotter,
I will get an ice cream,
It is getting late,
I have to go home now.

Hannah Day (10)
Alverstoke CE Junior School

ME IN THE SUMMER

In the summer I like to play,
I like to splash in the warm relaxing pool.
I put some suntan lotion on my clean, warm body.
I like to float in the water and sometimes, when
I float I begin to think that I am slowly sinking.
I like to sunbathe on my towel,
I even buy some cold food and cold drinks.

Louis Stacey (9)
Alverstoke CE Junior School

THE BEST HOLIDAY EVER IN SPAIN

Finally on holiday
In sunny Spain.
Down to the beach,
We got sunburnt,
Very, very bad.
Then we went swimming
In the sea,
After, straight back to the tent,
Ready for some entertainment.
I got hot,
So did Mum,
She started moaning,
So all the way back home we went,
With Mum still moaning!

Freya Griffin (10)
Alverstoke CE Junior School

THE FAIR

Down to the fair, *yippee*!
Buy some candyfloss, *yummy*!
Go to the haunted house, *scary*!
Up and down on the roller coaster, *ahh*!
Win a toy, *yess*!
On the merry-go-round, *wee*!
Screaming people, 'What a noise!'
Go on the big wheel, *ha ha*!
Going home, *yawn*!
Going to sleep, *Zzzzz*!

Mathew Saunders (10)
Alverstoke CE Junior School

IT'S BEHIND YOU!

If there was a monster behind you, would you know?
Are you sure you would know?
Really?
Now then, don't go and start believing that I'm a liar.
Look.
No not physically, just listen.
If there . . . what did you say?
Why am I edging away from you?
Oh just because . . .
What was I saying?
Oh yes, if there was a . . . er . . . well . . . er . . . a . . .
Monster behind you,
Then, er . . . well, you'd know wouldn't you?
Er . . . yes of course you would know!
No, don't look, what did I tell you?
I don't mean to alarm you but . . .
No!
I told you not to look.
Oh yes, I don't mean to alarm you but . . .
It's behind you!

Georgina Clark (10)
Alverstoke CE Junior School

FOOTBALL

The field is muddy,
I am cold and wet,
People shouting for the ball
Only ten yards away from the goal,
I have the ball by my feet,
I kick the ball,
It's a goal!

ᶜam Luce (9)
⸱rstoke CE Junior School

MY LITTLE BEAR

One day I opened my bedroom door
And there were paws upon my floor,
There stood a loving fluffy bear,
Wearing make-up on its hair.

My mum's making apple glump,
I showed the bear and heard a thump,
My mum had fainted on the ground,
Her eyes were spinning round and round.

It's nine o'clock, it's time for school,
My friends will think he's really cool,
The boys and girls were really scared,
They stood right back and then they glared.

I've learnt not to take him to school,
Although they think he's really cool.

Hannah Robertson (9)
Alverstoke CE Junior School

THE BIG SPHERE

One day a boy went out to play,
When he saw a comet coming his way,
Yet he didn't know what it was,
He said it was the Wizard of Oz.
Then it came closer and closer,
He was afraid he was going to be a roast dinner,
But then it popped right in front of him,
And all the rocks fell on him.
He played with the rock forever more,
That's why there's rocks on the floor.

Christopher Hough (10)
Alverstoke CE Junior School

MY TROMBONE

I took out a loan
To buy my trombone.

It's shiny and gold
And great to hold.

It has a big bell and slippery slide
And lots of saliva gets stuck inside.

I drain it out from time to time
Mum thinks it's disgusting but I think it's fine.

I'm in three bands
And Dad gives a hand.

He's just like a chauffeur
Though he lies on the sofa.

I enjoy my trombone
As I hope I have shown.

Owen Morgan (10)
Alverstoke CE Junior School

ON A RAINY AFTERNOON

The rain hasn't stopped all day
I'm looking out of the window
The sun has gone
There's nothing on TV
We've watched all our videos
We've eaten all our food
We can hear the foghorns beeping each other
There's lots of puddles.

Tommy Reed (9)
erstoke CE Junior School

THE ALLEY CAT

The alley cat walks around so proud,
Keeping his head off the ground.
The alley cat is silky black,
He makes his shadows on the wall.
They move and stretch both short and tall,
He eats whatever he can find,
Inside dustbins and behind.
Banana peels and apple cores,
Not very appetising at all.
Leftover turkey he has to eat,
At Thanksgiving it's his treat.
The alley cat has to sleep on the floor
    That's all there is,
        There isn't anymore.

Genevieve Price (9)
Alverstoke CE Junior School

ONE WHIMPERING WOODLOUSE

One wet whimpering woodlouse whining
Two tremendous trendy terriers,
Three throttling telescopes looking at the stars,
Four faithful fish fishing finely,
Five fantastic famous football stars,
Six slaves sweeping sadly,
Seven silly sausages sizzling sadly,
Eight enormous eggs looking out for elephants,
Nine knitting nannies knitting their knickers,
Ten tiny turtles trying to time.

Annalise Price (9)
Alverstoke CE Junior School

FROM NEXT-DOOR'S GARDEN

From next-door's garden, I heard a noise
And that noise I heard I thought was the boys
But it wasn't the boys
Because the boys were asleep.

While the boys were asleep
I heard a loud screech . . .
I was all of a quiver, shaking inside,
My heart, my lungs and also my liver,
I tried to be calm and not be alarmed.

Then the doorbell rang and I heard a great bang,
I opened the door and there I saw . . .
My mum looking at her swollen thumb.

Our cat had bitten her thumb so hard
And her thumb was very badly scarred.
She had hit her head on the door
And fallen over onto the floor.

We gave her some tea and sent her to bed
The cat came in and sat by the fire.
I told my dad I'd heard that noise
And he said you're a liar.

Elizabeth Allan (10)
Alverstoke CE Junior School

THE ALLEY CAT

The alley cat walked along the street,
Dirty paws, dirty feet,
I wonder if he's lonely out there,
I wonder where he sleeps,
I wonder if he likes me,
I wonder what he eats.

There're so many questions to ask,
I wish he'd answer them all,
We'll have to wait and see
If he comes to my door.

Sophie Hallett (10)
Alverstoke CE Junior School

MY METAPHORIC FAMILY

If I was a cartoon character
I would be Road Runner,
Fast, smart and funny.

If my sister was a TV star
She would be Willow,
Magical, attractive and nice.

If Mum was a Jedi
She would be Yoda,
Smart, ugly and slow.

If Dad was a teacher
He would be Mrs Butler,
Kind, helpful and the best.

If my other sister was an animal
She would be a headless chicken,
Wears glasses, funny and embarrassing.

If Max was a football player
He would be David Beckham,
Likes kicking, not smart and ugly.

If my brother was a wizard
He would be Harry Potter,
Dumb, tall and ugly.

Paul Nixon (9)
Alverstoke CE Junior School

LONELINESS

On my way to the beach, yip . . . spit!
Oh no, I'm stranded on the island, oh boy!
All alone, no one to play with!
It's very quiet, very peaceful!
I can hear squirrels chuckling, there's one, no two!
And coconuts crashing against each other, crack, yum, yum!
Birds singing, lovely sweet songs, how sweet!
And snakes, how bad!
Even whistling wind, I hear the breeze!
All the trees rustling!
I feel like going to sleep, good ni . . !

Boat's here, hooray!
On my way home, yippee!
Going to bed,
Falling to . . . *Zzzz*!

Robyn Bayles (9)
Alverstoke CE Junior School

THE LION

Yawning in the sun, the lion sleeps,
He suddenly twitches at the sound effects,
A group of antelope are drinking nearby.
He hides behind a clump of bushes that blend with his fur.
He pounces on his prey feeling good with himself.
He rips and tears at his prey,
He drags the dead body back to his cave,
The rest of the group go in a cloud of dust.
A tasty antelope . . .
Yum!
Roar!

Ian King (9)
Alverstoke CE Junior School

THE CAT DOWN MY ROAD

There's a cat down my road,
And you can't stroke it,
Because if you do it hisses at you,
It's a big cat, no doubt about that,
But it's fluffy,
And when it hisses its hair stands on end,
And you can see its sharp strong claws,
It jumps and its ears prick up!
Its mouth hangs open and you can see its teeth,
Pointy, shiny and large,
The cat down my road is fierce and frightening.

Isabel Davies (10)
Alverstoke CE Junior School

MY CREATURES POEM

One wiggly worm wiggling underground,
Two tiny toads turning a truck,
Three thugs looking through the thicket,
Four freaky frogs flying,
Five ferocious fighting flies,
Six smelly socks stinking,
Seven smelly stray snakes spitting slime,
Eight eggs eating,
Nine naughty knickers,
Ten terrible tigers talking to tortoises.

Alex Shaw (9)
Alverstoke CE Junior School

BIG LITTLE CATS

In the sunny savannah,
Lies a lioness and her cubs.
The cubs are playing joyfully
The mother is at rest.
The cubs tumble and pounce
The lioness lazily lies back
Shielding her eyes from the sun.
But the cubs carry on playing,
The sun gleams on their shiny brown coats
They are like bees around nectar
Waiting for their mother to hunt,
But their play fights and tumbles
Are like practise for the future.
While their mother chases buffalo
They stalk butterfly,
But they have a long way to go
Before they can hunt like their mother.

Jenny Tipton (9)
Alverstoke CE Junior School

MINIBEASTS

One wet woodlouse with wild woodpeckers,
Two tiny tigers trying to act tough,
Three frightened frogs forgetting to find their food,
Four fine fans, fanning faces fabulously,
Five frightened frogs flying down to Frigate farm,
Six silly snails slithering smartly,
Seven stinking skunks smelling sausages,
Eight enormous elephants eating eggs,
Nine naughty nanny goats nibbling nuts,
Ten tiny tadpoles talking to toadstools.

Rory Harper (10)
Alverstoke CE Junior School

TODAY'S THE DAY I WENT TO WORK

Today's the day I go to work,
With my mum and my uncle Kirk.
My mum said I had to be very good,
She said I really should,
But I just want to have some fun,
I want to jump and scream and run.

My mum left me at the reception desk,
With a small lady called Mrs Hesk,
The lady left me with some toys,
And said not to make any noise.
I sat there playing with the toys,
I wished there were some other boys.

There was a slam of a door,
Some footsteps down the corridor,
I had made it through that long day,
And all I had done was sit and play.
Today's the day I went to work
With my mum and my uncle Kirk.

Natalie James (10)
Alverstoke CE Junior School

A HOT DAY ON A DESERT ISLAND

I can hear singing birds.
I can see a screaming monkey that won't shut up.
I can hear old Red Indians shouting an old Indian song.
I can feel the howling wind hitting my face.
I can feel the sand on my feet.
I can see the lovely sun set on the horizon.
I can smell a cooked fish.

Michael Penfold (10)
Alverstoke CE Junior School

A Day At The Races

It was the most exciting day of my life,
I could not wait to see the race start.
The race started with the motors running,
You can hear the humming and buzzing of the engines,
Like mad, dashing and darting along the track.

With a puff of black smoke the car disappeared
And before you know you see it again.

He picks up speed so he can rush through the finish line,
The cheer goes up as he clutches the cup.

I was so happy when number eight won!

Philipa Wray (9)
Alverstoke CE Junior School

My Bedroom

My bedroom is a dizzy mess,
It's my own jumbled space,
My bed is like a lumpy island,
In a sea of hair stuff and sweet things.
I try so hard to keep my room tidy
But then Mum saves the day!
With her super-duper Dyson hoover,
But when I try, it's like there's a cloud of rain over me!
But sometimes my pet dog, Danny
Makes most of the mess when he wags his tail.

Elizabeth Hug (9)
Alverstoke CE Junior School

THE FIGURE

The figure is black from head to his toes
It has a camera hanging around his neck.
It sways around just like a bush,
Some people think he is, but I don't.

When I turn my light out it jumps at me
I give a shout, but nothing comes out,
I feel haunted.

I got into my duvet
And just when I was about to scream
I woke, it was a dream!

Alex Proudlock (9)
Alverstoke CE Junior School

HEAVEN OR HELL

Here lies the body of a man named Jin,
He went up to Heaven and he couldn't get in,
So he went down to Hell and he lived in a rotten cell,
And that was the end of him.

Down in Hell he started to despair,
'Cause all nasty stuff was there,
And he lived without a care,
The angel of Lord came down,
And teleported him to town,
He was free!

Max Ward (9)
Alverstoke CE Junior School

THE FRIDGE

The fridge is a monster
That gobbles up the food.

The fridge is a musician
That never breaks its tune.

The fridge is a ski slope
That never melts its snow.

The fridge is an extra sun
In case our sun runs out.

The fridge is a monster
That gobbles up the food.

Lauren O'Connor-Simpson (9)
Alverstoke CE Junior School

ONE WET WHALE . . .

One wet whale walking.
Two tiny tigers tracking tortoises.
Three thieves thinking thoughtful thoughts.
Four feathers falling from a fire.
Five faces face to face.
Six slimy slugs being sick.
Seven sad suns sucking the sky.
Eight eagles eating angels.
Nine naughty nannies knitting jumpers.
Ten tractors taking tortoises tacks.

Thomas Blackman (10)
Alverstoke CE Junior School

SPAIN

Sun caps, sun shades, vacation in Spain
The best holiday of the year
Packing the bags ready to go.
We're at the airport ready to go
We're going to Spain,
Jiggling and wiggling on aeroplane
Sprouts and roast chicken
There's still a way to go
We're landing at the airport, bump,
Spain, white beaches, bright blue sea,
Villa, Jacuzzi, come and see,
Sweltering sun, green palm trees.

Catherine Bednarski (9)
Alverstoke CE Junior School

A HOT DAY IN BARBADOS

It was a blazing day in Barbados
When I landed in the airport
A hot day in Barbados
You could see crabs in the water.
The air was getting hotter
Then I went to the beach
I had to put some cream on.
The ground was sweltering.
It was a busy day in the heart of Barbados.
The ground was getting hotter.

Sam Clulow (9)
Alverstoke CE Junior School

SONG

The black clouds are forming,
Soon the rain will fall.
My dear one is departing,
But please hear this call.
That always will I love you,
My one, my love, my all.
Forget all colours, wear only black,
Drink all the red wine off the rack.
Let his spirit live forever,
Don't let me think of him again, never.
He was my dark, my light,
My day and my night.
I loved him and that was all,
He was always there to catch me
Whenever I fall.

Ben Page (9)
Berrywood Primary School

THE HAUNTING

Under the covers, never asleep,
Afraid of a noise, the floorboards creak.
No one is here, there's hardly a sound,
A light flickers, then withers down.
A storm approaches, an almighty crack,
The shutters bang, wave and flap.
Step outside, the dark is daunting,
The words are whispered clear; *the haunting*.

Lisa Kilduff (10)
Berrywood Primary School

SPIDERS

Spiders are the tigers of the minibeast world,
Pouncing on any chance of a free meal.

Her web is like a gigantic bear trap,
Catching poor helpless flies as they buzz past.

Her eyes are like bowling balls gleaming in the sun,
Her legs are like lamp posts, long and spiky.

Her fangs are like butchers knives crushing all her prey,
The size of her makes me imagine what size would elephants be.

I wonder what it would be like being a spider at The Tate,
What does it feel like to have tiny ugly little humans walking
                              underneath you?

Joe Sheppard (11)
Berrywood Primary School

OURSELVES

O   ur bodies are important
U   seful and clever
R   ock hard like stones
S   ophisticated and smart
E   nergy absorbent
L   ots of limbs
V   ulnerable
E   ars are very sensitive
S   trong legs and fists.

Joe Janaway & David Gray (8)
Berrywood Primary School

WATER

Calm, peaceful waves hit very gently,
Like when you stroke a cat.
Rapidly waterfalls go crashing down,
As quick as you can say 'amazing'.

Through countryside it slowly trickles,
Noisy cows and horses love to see how it looks,
Like every person who sees this wonderful sight.
The brilliant thing it is, reflected like an extra big mirror.

Quiet streams, a boat can float on.
Fresh water as cold as can be ends up as a crashing sea.
Under the watery sea, bumpy coral appear to wave
The tranquil jellyfish rush past quickly.

Many people go to the beach and watch the drifting sand,
Calm, fresh, cool and smooth
Shivery water make people cold
But fish rush through like birds in the air.

Rebecca Sweet (8)
Berrywood Primary School

SONG

Stop all time, don't speak at all,
Don't let the children play with their ball.
Stop all the sorrow, stop all the pain,
Don't let me think of him ever again.

He was my light,
My life, my love and my might.
He was my soul, my spirit, my heart.
Why did God ever put us apart?

He was my colours,
Now he's gone everything's duller.
Lonely nights, lonely days,
We were together in so many ways.

Now he's dead,
I'll never find anyone else instead.
Someone please tell me why
He suddenly had to die?

Gareth Phillips (10)
Berrywood Primary School

SONG

Stop all the butterflies, stop all the bees,
Silence the birds singing in the trees.
Stop all songs of laughter and fun,
Take the clouds and the gleam of the sun.

Let the world stop spinning around,
As the coffin is buried in the ground.
Put all of the sparkling stars in a box,
Replace the green grass with rocks.

He was my wrong, he was my right,
He was my black, he was my white.
He was my morning, my noon, my night,
He was my loose, he was my tight.

I thought we were meant to be together,
I thought our time for separation would come never.
When I thought of you my heart burst with song,
I thought you would never leave. I was wrong.

Tiamanta Zacharias (10)
Berrywood Primary School

THE MAGIC WINDOW

Through the magic window I saw
Giant penguins, flying in the air,
Bugs the size of skyscrapers,
Someone swimming through a pool of money
And a tree made of gold.

Through the magic window I saw
A calculator with letters on,
A bridge made of paper,
A talking rock
And a flower made of stone.

Through the magic window I saw
A silver sun and a golden moon,
A tower of pizza,
A river of sand
And a fish walking on land.

Go and look out the magic window,
At least you'll see something.

Jack Hallett, Jennifer Blackwell (11)
& Rebecca Talbot, Tony Fudio, Chris Pye (10)
Berrywood Primary School

SONG

Stop the traffic, switch off the lights,
Silence the town, cancel the flights.
Cut off the power and make it be dark,
Put out the dog so I won't hear it bark.

Stop all the birds from overhead,
Make sure the children are all in bed.
Shut all the stores so we can't be fed,
Let all the people be dead.

She was my up, down, forward and back,
My bright and dark and my midnight black,
Now she's my star in the sky,
But I'm not ready to say goodbye.

Daniel Bradford (10)
Berrywood Primary School

SONG

Stop the day, the night, the sun, the rain,
The past, the future, the fun and the pain,
He was my left, my right, my high and low,
He was my love, my colour, my fast and my slow.

Stop the black, the white, my dark and light,
He was so fun until midnight.
He was my heart, my soul, my hello and bye bye,
He didn't deserve to go that high.

Stop the engines and the traffic lights,
Stop the holidays and the flights.
Stop the English and the maths,
Stop the calculations and the graphs.

Stop the bingo and the games,
Cover the pictures in their frames.
Stop the work and the meeting,
Stop the drinking and the eating.

The sun is not wanted now, put out the moon,
Take away the night and also the noon.
Cut down the trees and swallow the ocean,
My heart's overwhelmed with emotion.

Ross Wigley (10)
Berrywood Primary School

THE COLOURFUL DOOR

Go and open the scarlet door
    maybe outside there's a
    river of red roses
    rolling round in raspberry ripple ice cream.

Go and open the pink door,
    maybe outside there's a
    bundle of blooming blossoms bubbling
    with pink pollen.

Go and open the blue door,
    maybe outside there's a
    dolphin diving up and over the waves
    waggling its flippers in the sun.

Go and open the golden door,
    maybe outside there's a
    golden stream glimmering in the glistening
    sunshine glowing bright.

Go and open the green door,
    maybe outside there's a
    tornado of twirling twigs from the twisted trees
    turning in the wind.

Go and open the silver door,
    maybe outside there's a
    swirl of shimming colours, swirling silently
    like the snow.

Go and open the orange door,
    maybe outside there's a
    tree full of oranges, orang-utan or maybe even oak,
    that is overflowing, a magical garden.

Go and open the door,
     even if there's nothing there
     just go and open the door.

Victoria Salentino (10)
Berrywood Primary School

THE MOST IMPORTANT RAP

I am a cow,
I give milk to you,
Where would you be
If you didn't hear a moo?
If you didn't have me
What milk would you drink?
I'm most important, don't you think?

I am a bee,
I hate Winnie the Pooh,
If you take my honey,
I will sting you.
You should watch out,
I will always be near,
I'm the most important insect here.

I am a cat,
I like to purr.
If you come near me
You can touch my fur.
I am so pretty,
I can't bounce,
But I'm the most important animal to pounce.

Alice Gamble (8)
Berrywood Primary School

MAGIC BOX

In my box I will put
A sparkle from my mother's eyes
A shimmer from the sea at midnight
And a distant howl of the wind from yesterday.

In my box I will put
An animal from a far off land
A frozen pond with a glittering surface
And the fluffiest cloud in the sky.

In my box I will put
Sparkling jewels from an ancient land
A flower from last year's summer
And one of my dreams in a glass case.

In my box I will put
A swirling galaxy of colour of the rainbow
A shining star as bright as the moon
And the first drop of rain on a desert.

In my box I will put
The best days of my life all crammed into one
The rarest snakeskin saved forever
And a silver frog on a golden moon.

Carley Rowland (11)
Berrywood Primary School

THERE'S A SPIDER AT THE TATE

Her body is covered in black hair
From head to toe,
Each of her legs has its own spike to it,
Like a scorpion's tail.

Suddenly she moves, her leg twitches,
She even walks,
One leg at a time, slowly getting faster,
Suddenly it stops, it wasn't real.

Sophie Borrill (11)
Berrywood Primary School

SONG

Stop all the voices and
Shut down your brains.
Stop all the cars and
Stop all the trains.

Stop all the networks and
Stop all the birds.
Silence the teachers and
Quieten the kids.

Bring down the planes from
Swirling round.
But stop everything that
Lives on the ground.

Why did it have to happen
Like this?
The last thing he did was
Give me a kiss.

Will I ever see him again?
Will anything stop this
Terrible pain?

Zoe Harley (10)
Berrywood Primary School

THE MOST IMPORTANT RAP

I am a cow girl
On a horseback I ride.
I roam through the deserts
My horse is my pride.
I beat the Indians
With my arrows and my spears
And I'm the most important person here.

I am God
I hold people in my heart.
I love the earth,
We will never part,
I am powerful and I'm brave
Don't you fear,
So I'm the most important person here.

I am a tooth fairy,
I give you money.
Don't get tooth decay,
That's not funny.
I take your teeth,
I fly around at night.
So don't fall out with me or I'll win the fight.

Hannah Rood (8)
Berrywood Primary School

WEB WINDER

The spider is a web winder,
Winding webs high in the trees,
Ready to trap an unwary fly.

The spider is a web winder,
Winding webs, not knowing
when to spring the trap.

The spider is a web winder,
Winding webs, getting worked up,
When a fly flew into its web.

Cameron Hawkes (11)
Berrywood Primary School

THE MOST IMPORTANT RAP

I am a goldfish
I live in the sea
And some times in fish tanks
Where people feed me.
I'm small and long
And some things I fear,
I'm the most important animal here.

I am a rabbit
I hop up and down
And sometimes they keep me
And that's when I frown.
Sometimes people feed me
And in battles I flee,
The most important animal here is me.

I am a kitten
I like to purr
I like climbing trees
I have soft fur
I like to be fed
I'm afraid of deer,
I'm the most important animal here.

Lewis Matthews (8)
Berrywood Primary School

A Spider At The Tate

A spider is a predator, as scary as a bear,
Its legs are as tall as the Eiffel Tower,
The spider's head is as big as a beach ball,
The spider is as big as a jumbo jet,
The spider is a supernatural being,
The webs are as sticky as bubblegum stuck on the floor,
The webs are so gargantuan
They could wrap up the world.

Nic Illston (10)
Berrywood Primary School

There's A Spider At The Tate

Its legs are like a candle,
Ready to create an unexpected death
On the first living creature that she meets,
As she clumps along like a stampede
The world becomes empty
Because the few surviving humans
Scurry into their houses
Like ants into their sand made hills.

Matthew Luke (10)
Berrywood Primary School

There's A Spider At The Tate

There's a spider at The Tate, big, black and tough.
She wanders in the night like a moving tower block.
If you see her it's like a dark never-ending dream.
If you go under her you'll see her hostile young.
The monstrous roar lets you know she's at The Tate.

Seb Smith (10)
Berrywood Primary School

THE COLOURFUL DOOR

Go and open the blue door,
maybe you'll see
a calm sea, a bright sky
or a winding river
glinting in the sun.

Go and open the green door,
maybe you'll see
a field of grass, a slimy toad
or a giant oak tree
swaying in the wind.

Go and open the yellow door,
maybe you'll see
a giant sunflower, a shining sun
or a swarm of bees
busily collecting pollen.

Go and open the red door,
maybe you'll see
a colourful parrot, a prickly red rose
or a great flame
signalling danger.

Go and open the white door,
maybe you'll see
a snowy mountain, a fluffy cloud
or a white horse
galloping in the blowy wind.

Go and open the black door
and even if there is only darkness
at least there'll be
some sort of colour.

Alec Howlett (10)
Berrywood Primary School

SCHOOL DAYS

Oh no, it is another day,
Get out of bed, OK, OK,
Going though the old school gate,
Oh no again, I am late.
Going in the miserable hall,
It makes me feel really small.
Now it's recess, hip, hip hooray,
Let's go outside and play.
Back to work, it's really boring,
I feel like sleeping and snoring.
There goes that bell again,
Lunch is here yet again.
School dinners are a load of slop,
And you don't get alot!
The gravy is really thick,
Yuk! I feel really sick.
Back to the class, I'm feeling fine,
Because it is nearly home time.

Aimee Parrett (9)
Crofton Anne Dale Junior School

AUTUMN

Leaves falling
Morning dawning
Sun shining
Silver lining
Children go la-la
Sheep go ba-ba
Children running
Foxes cunning.

Laura Farmer (8)
Crofton Anne Dale Junior School

THE FOUR SEASONS

When the wind blows, the trees move to and fro,
When the sun shines, things begin to grow,
In the winter some birds go away,
In the spring they come back to stay,
In the autumn and winter the animals prepare
For the spring and the summer when young ones appear.

Aisha Livingstone (10)
Crofton Anne Dale Junior School

THE SWAN

Glides gracefully over untouched waters
Arching his neck like church doors
Proud and vain he elegantly stretches
Stepping cautiously out of swan filled lakes
Eyeing visitors as they point unneedingly
Waiting to attack and peck unwanted visitors.

Lindsey Rossell (11)
Crofton Anne Dale Junior School

INDIA

The floods have hit a country
Which seems like a million miles away
Devastating families
Lay there as they pray
All the little children lying in the streets
Dying of starvation
While others sit and eat.

Giuliette Catterson-West (11)
Crofton Anne Dale Junior School

THE KITTEN

She is as black as night,
Has sparkly green emerald eyes.

Dazzling in the moonlight,
Quiet as a mouse.

Fluffy round ball,
Sleeps in the sunshine.

Looks for food in the jungle
While pouncing proudly.

Rolling round,
Trying to catch aeroplanes in the garden.

Trying to catch a ball of string,
But keeps kicking it away from him.

Kittens kick kindly to their owners.

Natalee Hunt (9)
Crofton Anne Dale Junior School

NIGHT

Trying desperately to comfort you
Her calm bright red eyes drag you to her warmth
Her smiling rose lips make you know she is gentle
Her long brown hair tells you there's no harm
You'd want to cuddle her for she wears golden fur.

She moves slowly so you can capture her sweet dreams
She makes you feel safe taking baby steps in your head
And then your dreams will dance with her.

Sarah Hicks (11)
Crofton Anne Dale Junior School

THE SUN

The sun is like a gigantic ball of fire
Hanging from a long, long wire,
Keeps us warm, keeps us bright,
Never shines in the middle of the night.

Sometimes you can get burnt by the sun,
Then it does not seem like fun.

Matthew Swann (8)
Crofton Anne Dale Junior School

POLAR BEAR

White, fuzzy and cold,
Strolling around on the ice,
Big, huge furry paws
Covering up his black nose
And rolling around in snow!

Jenna Lloyd (10)
Crofton Anne Dale Junior School

A HOT DAY

Blistery blazing heat.
Sand so hot it burns your feet.
Sparkly glittering yellow sand.
The sea is just a blue band.
Birds fly over with their feathery wings.
In the distance the moon sings.
Another day, another night,
Will it be hot tomorrow?

Samantha Drain (8)
Crofton Anne Dale Junior School

HOME SWEET HOME

No! I don't want people in me!
I want to stay empty!
I want to be peaceful, quiet, silent.
I like the mice running around, scampering and playing.
I don't like naughty children thundering down the stairs
                              that echo around me
Or the slamming of the doors!
I like the wind that howls around me at night,
When it's dark, cold and spooky.
The creaking of the doors, the wind blowing through,
Like a ghost brushing and floating past me.
I don't like the ear-splitting music,
The pounding on the walls and the children that yell and bawl.
I want to be tranquil and calm and left on my own.

Christopher Solly (9)
Crofton Anne Dale Junior School

WOLF

Standing alone on top of the prairie, dead of night
As the moon shines its beams.
The light peeps through the tall conifers
And her shadow on the hill leans.
Her cry for a mate echoes in the valley below
And her grey rough coat blows in the wind.
The long grass around her moves slow
The mountains behind her are low
As she howls every night and just stands there still . . .
Waiting for company.

Emma Bailey (11)
Crofton Anne Dale Junior School

MY HAIRDRESSER'S AN ALIEN

I can almost swear
That my hairdresser's an alien!
Although she does my hair
I can see through her!

The blaster gun that shoots out air
The surgical tools they use . . .
And although she neatly does my hair
I know her plan . . .

The mirrors and the swivel chair
Are actually control pads
Where she neatly does my hair
I've seen it!

The squeezy bottle that she uses,
Is full of goo and it oozes . . .
And although she neatly does my hair
I have to stop her!

Terri Witherden (11)
Crofton Anne Dale Junior School

THE BLACK PANTHER

It creeps through the hidden woods,
His radar scanning the forest, freaking out his prey.
His roar screeches down your spine
                        like icy cold flint.
His claws as hot as burning firewood,
He strikes into his enemy's heart,
The eerie silence stretched right across the forest.
He moves on, scanning his radar once more.

Simon Pinhorne (10)
Crofton Anne Dale Junior School

THE MERMAID

I was down by the seaside building a sandcastle,
When my sister called. I was sad to go home.
Later that night I went down to see my castle.
When I got there a lady was sitting down,
But this lady had a tail with flippers,
She was a mermaid.
She was sad, 'I beg you to help me with my family because . . .'
The moon stopped glowing, the sun rose and she was gone,
She whispered from the sea,
'You won't tell anyone I'm here, will you.'
To this day I have never seen her again.

Laura Phillips (9)
Crofton Anne Dale Junior School

NIGHT

Night is growing, tiptoeing nearer,
Comforting us, gliding closer.
She sings her soothing song.
Her long jet-black hair flowing over the lost traveller,
Giving them hope.
Her long gown sweeping the ground,
Flowing sleeves and delicate fingers shoot out sweet dreams.
Her night's work done,
She carries on her journey around the world.

Emily Smith (10)
Crofton Anne Dale Junior School

MY CAT

My cat loves to catch rabbits,
He can't stop it,
It's a habit.
He is as black as coal,
He even chases moles down a hole,
When he's asleep
He's a great big heap.
He loves his food
But sometimes he is in a mood,
But I love him all the same.

Gemma Truslove (9)
Crofton Anne Dale Junior School

I'VE GOT A DOG

I've got a dog
He's a bit like a frog
He leaps about
Without any doubt
He barks really loud
But I'm not proud
He's a really fast eater
He races around like a cheetah
But at the end of the day
I get my way.

Daniel Gordon (8)
Crofton Anne Dale Junior School

THE SIMPSONS

Let me introduce you to the Simpsons
They are all very funny
Let's take Maggie for example,
She loves to suck her dummy.

There's very clever Lisa
She always gets an 'A'
She works just like a busy bee
That's all she does all day.

With hair as spiky as a hedgehog
Is a dude by the name of Bart
He gets into all kinds of trouble
When he steals Squishes from the Kwik-E-mart.

Homer's the dad of the family
His belly is very round
He loves to eat lots of donuts
And say 'Doh! I've put on some pounds!'

And finally there is the mum
Her Christian name is Marge
She stores lots of things in her hair
Which is bright blue and very large.

Curtis Barber (9)
Crofton Anne Dale Junior School

THE LUNAR ECLIPSE
(9th January 2001)

We stood out on our porch.
It was hard to see the moon, so we headed to the sea with our torch.
We parked by the shore,
Eager to see more.
It took several hours of our time,
Until the sun, Earth and moon were eventually in line.
Although it was a starry night,
Several clouds came into sight.
Our view was briefly obscured
But the dazzling effect was hardly flawed.
That beautiful sight out over the sea,
Is something that will stick in my memory.
We were just thinking of going back,
When finally it all went black.
The reflection from the Earth's atmosphere,
Created a halo around the moon, so clear!
Its reddy, yellow hew,
Was watched by us and our companions, surprisingly few.
Time to go home,
Feeling strangely alone.
Time for bed,
And to try and clear the exciting thoughts from my head!

Samuel Shears (9)
Crofton Anne Dale Junior School

A Day At The Circus

Tamers-whipping
Acrobats-flipping
Rope walkers-walking
People-talking
Announcers-announcing
Lions-pouncing
Monkeys-cycling
Sweeties-crunching
Mouths-munching
Clowns-performing
Children-laughing
Crowds-crying
Hot dogs-disappearing
Chips-appearing
Coke-going
Beer-flowing
Trampolinists-flying
Dare devils-leaping
Toddlers-waking
Audience-clapping
Circus-ending.

Angus Ewen (9)
Crofton Anne Dale Junior School

Night

I met at night the Queen of Night
She has still a kind face,
She took a slow pace across the valley steep.

Her dark sparkled dress followed her
Whilst her dark silk hair flew in the air
And her round crown brightened up the night.

Whilst she took a slow step across the sky
Her haunted castle awaited her,
The foggy walls were as black as night.

Her thousands of sparkling eyes
Are adored by the thousands of children who watch her
Whilst they fall into deep dreams.

Emma Ponting (10)
Crofton Anne Dale Junior School

ANGEL

I am an angel
I go to battle
Against *Satan.*

I do not need the sword
I am the sword
I do not need the fire
I am the fire.

We are the stars
We are the daylight
We are the sun
So the day is light for you
But is not for us.

I am the sword
I am the fire
I am the night sky
I am the stars
I am the daylight
I am the sun

I am an angel.

Katie McBride (10)
Crofton Anne Dale Junior School

THE ISLAND

There's a small blue fishing boat
Moored up to the side,
There's a sandy, golden beach
Waiting to welcome you.
Then a steep grassy green bank
Silently challenges you.
Waving grasses,
Guiding you home
To the island.

Red and yellow oak trees
Waving in the wind,
Pale creamy apple blossom
Beckons you towards it,
Yellow hazy meadows
Whisper out a whispered song
And a gurgling brook
Leads you home
To the island.

Emma Burton (10)
Crofton Anne Dale Junior School

SUMMER

Distant trees sway in the warm wind
It blows across woods and meadows
Birds hover on the gentle breeze
And sing sweetly in the gardens.
Rays of sunshine brighten up the day
And children laugh with joy.

Rachael Farmer (10)
Crofton Anne Dale Junior School

THE DAY I WENT TO SEA

I went to sea in a rowing boat
I was splashed by the slaughtering waves
The sea was a deadly fish last night
Hitting us with its lethal tail.

The sea was like a monster
Which made our boat capsize
The sea was a giant blue balloon last night
Popping when it hurled us into the air.

The sea was tough and rough last night
But when morning was nigh
The fish sank heavily beneath the waves
And the monster fell dreamily beneath the sand.

Laurence Coulton (9)
Crofton Anne Dale Junior School

A BONFIRE

A bonfire is like a lion roaring and moving side to side.
The wooden sticks are the bones of his prey.
Cinders fly out like they have been fired from a gun.
The smoke is a cheetah kicking up dust as it runs.
Without a warning the flames shoot up and die back down.
The flames are like a molten lava monster roaring at the
                              crowd of people.
Gradually the flames die down as the lion falls asleep.
The ashes are the lion fading away.

Andrew Woods (8)
Crofton Anne Dale Junior School

LUXURY ISLAND

Few ships have made it to this island
We may be the first?
Who knows, our boat may not make it?
This luxury island may disappear
But, where would it go?

I'm on a voyage to a sandy island
Where sugar plum trees grow,
We hope we get there soon
On this luxury island.

Motionless blue seas, with exotic fish
Rocky mountains, with bright trees
Fruit that swims and flows through streams,
With a sun that makes smiles beam
The azure sky as strong as stone
This island, we hope we get there soon.

The plants and flowers are luxurious,
The mind-bending flower,
Which makes you feel dazed,
They grow in the sea, and on land
The bright colours will light up your life.

The wild creatures how different they are,
With curly faces and sparkling tails,
This land is full of different things
Animals live naturally like we do,
They are all different, with their own habitat,
Our boat may get there soon.

The stars twinkle at night
While the moon lights up the island,
You won't need a fire
As the sky will light you up,
The fire beetle will let you play
On this luxury island.

Helen Selby (11)
Crofton Anne Dale Junior School

MAGIC FROG

I am a magic frog
All green with black spots
I live by myself under a log
Where it doesn't get too hot.

Here I am sitting still
Waiting for the sun to rise.
When it does from above the hill
I'll be a little more wise.

Now I am in the sunshine
For the world to see
Waiting patiently for the night-time
Hoping for someone to come and play with me.

Soon out of the blue
A boy with a stick appears
Up and down the road he goes
Waiting for me to near.

My time is up for the day
I've had my time to play
As I go back under my log
I am still a magic frog.

Grant O'Neill (9)
Crofton Anne Dale Junior School

OUR DOGS

Nina is nimble, Nina is quick
She is small and black and very slick.
She likes to run, she likes to play
And lives to sit in the sun all day.

Ezza is black and white and tan
He's full of muscle, a real strong man.
He chases a ball and never lets go
Whether you are a friend or foe.

Mica is golden, we call her a horse
She really is a dog of course.
She loves to retrieve things from the sea
She brings things to Dad, to Mum and me.

Cassie's black coat is silken and glossy
She is very sweet but tends to be bossy.
When out for a walk she loves to run fast
The other dogs she loves to run past.

Bonnie is a puppy, all fur and skin
Waiting for her body to grow in.
She's full of fun and skids and skates
She likes to rough and tumble with her mates.

Ashleigh Carter-Hearn (10)
Crofton Anne Dale Junior School

THE BIN LINER

The black bin liner is a bat
swooping through the trees
A black hole that sucks in everything
that even comes near
A mine that goes
>   down
>   down
>   down . . .
An empty space in your mind
Carbon loosened up by being zero
>   below
That thing under the sofa
A warp hole going from one place to another
A lifeless blob, a black slime
>   oozing into your shoes.

Chay Paterson (10)
Crofton Hammond Junior School

ORANGE IS . . .

Orange is the hot sun
burning fiercely in the sky
Orange is the flickering fire
that burns harshly in the forest
Orange is a juicy fruit
that squelches in the kitchen
Orange is a hungry tiger roaring
loudly in the jungle
Orange is a beautiful star
twinkling brightly in the night sky.

Hannah Vardy (9)
Crofton Hammond Junior School

THE BLACK BIN LINER IS . . .

The black bin liner is a kite
flying in the air

The black bin liner is a cat's coat
shining in the moonlight

The black bin liner is a gigantic
black hole

The black bin liner is a vampire's cape
swishing in the wind

The black bin liner is a bat
hanging upside down on a tree

The black bin liner is the night sky
shining with all the stars

The black bin liner is a blackboard
smudged with chalk

The black bin liner is a butterfly
sitting on a flower

The black bin liner is a crow
pecking worms out of the ground

The black bin liner is a black tunnel
that has no way out

The black bin liner is a field
full of sheep running all around.

Sarah Revill (9)
Crofton Hammond Junior School

THERE'S A MONSTER

There's a monster
A monster
It's in my bed.

Creeek
Huh, he's coming closer
Crack
Turn on the light.

There's a monster
A monster
It's in my bedroom.

Rustle
Huh, what's he doing
Rumble
Turn on the light.

There's a monster
A monster
It's in my bedroom.

Thud
Huh, he's moving
Scrape
Turn on the light.

There's a monster
A monster
It's in my bedroom.

James Marlow (10)
Crofton Hammond Junior School

SILVER

Stars are shiny, they twinkle brightly in the sky
Ice is slippery, it glimmers coldly on the lake
Moon is shiny, it gleams shinely in space
Waves are cold, they crash roughly in the seas
Snow is freezing, it sparkles softly in the back garden
Sea shells are smooth, they make a sweet noise on the beach.

Kathryn Blainey (9)
Crofton Hammond Junior School

WHITE

White is a soft dove gliding calmly in the bright sky
White is beautiful snow drifting from the clouds above
White is a daisy peacefully swaying in the whistling wind
White is a cloud moving slowly in the grey sky
White is fresh milk from a cow dripping slowly into a mug
White is ice freezing a shiny lake.

Hannah Meonch (9)
Crofton Hammond Junior School

ORANGE

Orange is a shiny sun glowing fiercely in the sky
Orange is a juicy orange squirting frantically in the kitchen
Orange is a scaly goldfish that swims quickly in its tank
Orange is a raging fire flickering ferociously in the dry wood
Orange is crunchy autumn leaves falling lightly from a tree
Orange is a vicious tiger pouncing gracefully on its prey.

Laura May (9)
Crofton Hammond Junior School

In The Ocean

The waves crashing in the breeze,
swishing and swaying like the wind.
The seagulls squeaking and squawking
for something to eat.
The ocean waves swaying from side to side,
not having a very good ride.
The ocean waves are playing chase,
going at their own pace
The waves crashing in the breeze,
swishing and swaying like the wind.
The seagulls squeaking and squawking
for something to eat.

Hannah Teasdale (9)
Crofton Hammond Junior School

Red Is . . .

Red is a burning fire that flickers fiercely
on Guy Fawkes Night,
Red is the scorching sun that shines in the sky,
Red is a colourful poppy that sits in a pot,
Red is a moody crab that snaps its claws
stressfully on the beach,
Red is a scrumptious strawberry
slowly growing in the ground,
Red is a curvy starfish that swims in the sea.

Sophie Hodges (10)
Crofton Hammond Junior School

SPLASHING, CRASHING WAVES

Splashing, crashing waves
Lashing against the shore
Splashing, crashing waves
Dashing about some more.

Shoals of silver fish
Swimming in the sea
Super, shiny starfish
Looking right at me.

Splashing, crashing waves
Lashing against the shore
Splashing, crashing waves
Dashing about some more.

Dazzling, dainty dolphins
Diving deep below
Dazzling, dainty dolphins
Further down they go.

Abi Philo (10)
Crofton Hammond Junior School

THE BIN LINER

The bin liner is . . .

A dark, gloomy tunnel
A thick piece of chocolate
A huge slab of tar
A soft, furry cat's tail
A dreamy night sky
A spooky haunted house
or just a bin liner.

Dulcie Allen (10)
Crofton Hammond Junior School

THE BOX

The brown box is . . .
A small, peaceful cottage with shiny windows
and a huge front door
A ferocious racing car that zooms ahead of all the rest
It could be the box that contains a funny clown-like head
and jack-in-a-box body
Or a tank that glows as it goes into battle
The box could be the head of Frankenstein
that is covered with nuts and bolts
A shop full of hand-crafted toys and lovely sweets
The box could be a secret place where you can hide
but just your face
The box can be many things you see
The box can be whatever you want it to be.

Matthew Pearson (10)
Crofton Hammond Junior School

THE BLACK BIN LINER

The black bin liner is . . .
A witch's cape flapping around in the breeze
A deep, dark, black hole
A kite flying around in the air
A squawking crow
A black witch's cat
A firework zipping around in the dull sky
A parachute floating down to earth
A greasy old oil slick
A ghost flying about.

Adam Foster (10)
Crofton Hammond Junior School

RED

Red is a fiery fire crackling frantically in the forest
Red is flowing blood rushing pacily in the body
Red is a shiny postbox in London
Red is a twinkling bus driving madly at the bus stop
Red is a noisy fire engine extinguishing fires
rapidly at the fire station
Red is a stinging rose swaying perfectly in the field.

Josh Read (10)
Crofton Hammond Junior School

MY POEM ABOUT WHITE

White is snow floating in a cold breeze
White is milk spilt on a road, coming out gently
White is a polar bear playing carefully with its friend
White is a unicorn galloping in a dream
White is glue sticking roughly to paper
White is talcum powder going on your skin
White is chalk scratching on a board.

Chlöe Smith (9)
Crofton Hammond Junior School

WEATHER CHANGE

W hining winds wailing
E ndless echoes around
A nimals ambling for food
T hundering echoes, tumbling trees
H uge hailstones hammering
E verlasting errors
R ivers raving.

Kirsty Veitch (10)
Crofton Hammond Junior School

ORANGE

Orange is a bumpy orange
rolling softly on the table
Orange is a fiercely shiny sun
glowing in the sky
Orange is a scaly goldfish
that swims quickly in its fish tank
Orange is an enormous fire flickering
spitefully in a dry wood
Orange is some autumn leaves
falling lightly from a tree
Orange is Tigger that is soft
and bounces happily in the jungle.

Sophie Norris (9)
Crofton Hammond Junior School

YELLOW

Yellow is the steamy sun that
glows proudly in the sky
Yellow is the rough sand that
glistens happily at the seaside
Yellow is a squishy banana that
squelches in a fruit bowl
Yellow is a sour lemon that
squirts rapidly in the drink of coke
Yellow is a juicy melon that
dribbles slowly on someone's chin
Yellow is a golden daffodil that
swishes rapidly in a garden.

Emma Gibb (10)
Crofton Hammond Junior School

THE TOILET

In the toilet I hear gurgles
In the toilet I hear sludge
In the toilet I see ripples
In the toilet I see gunge

Sucking down my wastage
Washing it away
You can hear it flushing
I do it every day

Washing my hands after
Rinsing off the germs
Pulling out the plughole
Sloshing it away

In the toilet I hear gurgles
In the toilet I hear sludge
In the toilet I see ripples
In the toilet I see gunge.

Esther Main (10)
Crofton Hammond Junior School

GRASPING GREEN

Green is soft grass which grows in a field
Green is a straight tree that grows in a forest
Green is a slippery eye which lets you see
Green is a prickly bush that grows in your garden
Green is a horrible crocodile which eats people.

Harry Ramshaw (9)
Crofton Hammond Junior School

BLACK, TERRIBLE BLACK

Black is fierce storm clouds looming tensely
on a freezing, cold day
Black is unknown space, it stays still naturally
in the dark sky
Black is a tiny bat that whistles through the air

Black is death, horrible death that strikes suddenly
anywhere . . . anywhere . . . anywhere
Black is the night, the dark night that stares
endlessly . . . endlessly . . . endlessly
Black is a bruise, a painful bruise that darkens
slowly . . . slowly . . . but surely.

Philip Tyreman (10)
Crofton Hammond Junior School

FUNFAIR

F   izzing, fuzzing fireworks
U   nder the clouds they boom!
N   ever ending Catherine wheels, flashing lights they zoom!
      The rides twirl and twist like a dizzy ballerina
      The children scream and shout with a never ending stop!
F   lashing flying roundabouts
A   ching headaches start to come
I   n the ghost tunnel children screech and wail
R   unning about having so much fun, yet knowing a lot more to come!

Fiona Riches (10)
Crofton Hammond Junior School

BLUE

Blue is a sunny sky that shines brightly
Blue is a swishy sea that sways calmly on the beach
Blue is a silky whale that swims in the sea
Blue is squelchy wellingtons that walk heavily on the ground
Blue is two shining eyes
Blue is wrinkling, rippling water spraying out the tap.

Elena Wason (9)
Crofton Hammond Junior School

INSIDE THE TOMB OF SILENCE

Inside the tomb of silence
I could smell nothing but dust
Dust tickling up my nose
As if it were a *feather!*

Inside the tomb of silence
I felt remarkable
Never have I seen something
So fascinating . . . *beautiful!*

Inside the tomb of silence
I could see gold necklaces
That look like fairy chains
Gold animals as long as
Nile crocodiles!

Inside the tomb of silence
Stood two pure gold
Marvellously built statues
They looked like they were guarding
The *treasure!*

Georgia Bergmann (8)
Grange Junior School

TUTANKHAMEN'S TOMB

As I peered through the hole I could see the sight of glimmering gold in
my eyes
The glint made me sort of blind
I had to dig right through the first door
As I did I saw more and more of the antechamber
But I ain't seen nothing yet
As I entered the third doorway I found Tutankhamen's body
The head was clean shaven, his eyelashes were super long
and his skull was empty
But that was just the sarcophagus
The most precious treasure was the death mask
Some believe it, some don't
It smelt really musky with beetles everywhere
I lifted the lid of the sarcophagus and yanked it off
Then I lifted the coffin lid off and there he was!

David Rae (9)
Grange Junior School

TUTANKHAMEN'S TOMB

As I made the hole bigger, I began to feel excited
I saw the amazing mask as gold as the sun
The shining cow head, smooth and glimmering
The tomb of Tutankhamen has come alive
And everything was silent apart from death music
The room glitters like the stars and moon at night
Blinding gold in cases of rock solid glass
It smells like smelly food rotting over the many years
Amazing statues with gold covering them brilliantly
But still amazing things are everywhere.

Amy Brown (8)
Grange Junior School

IN THE ANTECHAMBER

As I went into the antechamber I heard a bang
And I smelt dust and it went up my nose
I felt a rusty wall
I saw the jewels of Tutankhamen
I saw the hieroglyphics
The death mask was used for Tutankhamen's head
It has a long beard
The whole death mask is gold and blue
Tutankhamen's lips are red
His eyes are dark blue
His eyebrows are dark blue too
At the back of the death mask is hieroglyphics.

Jodie Stewart (8)
Grange Junior School

THE ANTECHAMBER

The gold was bright as I peeked
The glint of gold everywhere around
I could see a golden statue
I could see a golden bench
I could hear creaks
Creak of wood
I could hear echoes
Echoes of whetstones
I'm feeling frantic
Frantic feeling
I feel shocked
Shocked like lightning.

Shane Atkinson (8)
Grange Junior School

SIGHT AND HOWARD CARTER

Sight

The gold in the night light
shivering in the tomb
The hole in the ground
with crawling creatures.

Howard Carter

I was going crazy
but discovered a pharaoh
The discovery was bonkers
with a destruction
The pharaoh is bare
then embalmed.

Wayne Peake Junior (9)
Grange Junior School

STEP TO THE TOMB

I was full of excitement but I was scared as well
But wait, what's this? A step, ah, I will call Lord Carnarvon
Lord Carnarvon came straight away
We were really nervous.

As we found more steps we got more excited and nervous
In twenty-four more days we found the antechamber
Twenty-seven days and we found the fourth doorway
But we all feel strange . . .
Almost as if we've been
Cursed!

Christie Lockley (8)
Grange Junior School

GOING THROUGH THE TOMB

As I made the hole in the door
I began to feel very excited
I could see statues and gold
Everywhere the glint of gold

I managed to get through the door
And as I did I could see
Statues of animals and gods
All decorated with some gold

I could see boxes and chains and vases
All decorated with a bit of gold
I could see straw and sand bags and baskets
All decorated with a bit of *gold!*

I feel absolutely wonderful and so excited
I feel so relieved but a bit worried
I feel so magnificent and also delighted
I feel happy but also worried

I feel so surprised and so shocked
I feel so nervous and *worried!*

Kirsty Hambrook (9)
Grange Junior School

TUTANKHAMUN'S TOMB

As I found the first step, then another . . .
Then a tomb! I've found the great Tutankhamun
I've found him after all these years
I've found him with all his treasures
I am going to be rich because
I found Tutankhamun's golden death mask.

Ben Gosling (8)
Grange Junior School

THE ANTECHAMBER

The smell is comforting
Dust tickling up my nose
As if it were a feather
Incense is burning . . .

But
The whole room is glittering
Glittering with glamour -
As glittery as sunshine
But, incense is still burning . . .

Burnished animals;
As long as a Nile crocodile
The glint of rubies in my eyes
And yet incense is *still* burning . . .

Everything's glamour
Everything's splendour
But everything catches
My eye.

Rebekha Maskell (8)
Grange Junior School

THE DISCOVERY OF TUTANKHAMUN

I was wild and scared
It was like being in a dragon's cave
Then I found a hole and made it bigger
I found some steps and went down them
The last step creaked and I was scared
Suddenly a light twinkled into my eyes
The light was bright and shiny like a real diamond
It shone upon a pile of rocks.

Gemma Brown (8)
Grange Junior School

SECRET

My friend told me a secret
She said I had to keep it
She uttered a word which I didn't hear
I could sense her strong flavour of fear
I could feel her leaking tears on my cheek
She looked like a rag doll, all helpless and weak
She screamed and wailed out in pain
She said 'I haven't told you this before'
But she left it there and said no more
For her dad was there in his pick-up truck
He signalled and said for her to hurry up
She whispered through her tears 'Hospital'
And suddenly I felt a surge of pain
And I was struck yet again
I woke up lying next to her hospital bed
'I had an operation, what happened to you? she said
Her secret is now locked in my heart
And will stay there forever more . . .

Avital Halpin (11)
Highfield CE Primary School

LONELY

Here in my house weeping,
Here in my house thinking,
Here in my house grieving,
Here in my house dreaming,
Of how my life could be.

In my house no one who cares,
In my house no one to share my thoughts,
In my house no one and nothing to love.

Here in my house feeling lonely,
Here in my house feeling rejected,
Here in my house feeling upset,
I wish, and wish but it doesn't change a thing.

Here in my house abandoned,
Here in my house not wanted,
Here in my house I just want to die . . .

Here in my house.

Becca Carozzi (11)
Highfield CE Primary School

THE FRIGHT

The other night I had a fright
I turned to the left then the right
I quivered and shivered all over my body
I climbed out of bed and stepped on poor Noddy
So I went downstairs and turned on the telly,
In the corner of the room was an old smelly welly,
So I went to the fridge and found some leftover jelly.
I went back upstairs keeping close to the wall
So nothing would grab me and drag me to their hole.
Ghosts going through my head and into my mind,
Sucking my blood all out of my brain.
He stopped for a moment and went to the phone,
Calling his mates for a revolting smell and to chew on my bones
Turning round in my bed I banged my head
I quickly sat up: and fell out of bed.
Only then did I realise how silly I'd been,
The thoughts in my head had all been a dream.

Matthew Childs (9)
Highfield CE Primary School

BULLIES

I'm walking along on a dreary school morning
Trying to be very late
Trying to not see
The people that I hate.

I get to the gate
Nobody's there
They're probably wondering
'Where is she, where?'

It's not because they're kind
They just want to be hurtful
I can't wait till I go home
Where I can rest and be peaceful.

I walk into the classroom
They gave me a look
Their faces seemed to say
'I'm go'na get you, you're not let off the hook!'

Why are there bullies?
Why can't it be fair?
But I can't stand up to *them*
I wouldn't dare!

Lucy Argall (9)
Highfield CE Primary School

CATS

Cats are clever, hate foul weather
Stay in when it's wet, go out when it's dry,
They huddle right by the fire,
Stretch and purr, what a life for a cat.

Sarah Aitchison (9)
Highfield CE Primary School

THE THINGS I DO

On Monday
I run to pretty Gosport quickly
I get up from my warm bed early
Monday is a good day

On Tuesday
I play with my brown dog nicely
I snore in my big bed crazily
Tuesday is a nice day

On Wednesday
I cycled to nice Southampton slowly
I sail my boat to unlucky Isle of Wight boringly
Wednesday is an outing day.

On Thursday
I licked my orange lolly peacefully
I became ill in my big bed sadly
Thursday is a sad day.

On Friday
I sold my big cat Riddy
I hugged my thin mum lovingly
Friday is a cool day.

On Saturday
I wore my brown coat proudly
I ate my curly spaghetti hungrily
Saturday is a groovy day.

On Sunday
I sat on my small chair lonely
I did my white homework boringly
Sunday is a boring day.

Natalie Fuller (9)
Marycourt School

Two Sides Of The Sea

I go sailing on a sailing boat,
It sits upon the sea.
Upon the little waves that are silky and shiny
On the cold sea I sail through the ocean,
All silvery as the sun shines down making the boat glow.
It is relaxing, with the gentle rippling, swishing in my ears,
I love this sound of the sea,
It is so calming.

But then;
Violent storms are rushing through the ocean,
The sea is rough, it is noisy and windy,
The boat crashes against the white horses,
And there's a terrible fright to all the sailors.
The waves are rough and gigantic,
Made by the fierce and freezing wind
Oh how I wish the sea was calm
And I could relax once more.

Josephine Durham (8)
Marycourt School

Colours

Red is a phone box,
Red is a soldier,
Red is a postbox,
Red is my favourite car.

Blue is a table,
Blue is a bag,
Blue is a jumper,
Blue is my favourite lorry.

Yellow is a sun,
Yellow is a banana,
Yellow is a daffodil,
Yellow is my favourite train.

Green is a tree,
Green is some grass,
Green is some bushes,
Green is my favourite bus.

Harry Eastman (8)
Marycourt School

VALENTINES ON THE SEA

The sea was calm,
The sea was silky,
The sea was lovely and gentle,
The sea was relaxing and romantic.

The sea was rough,
The sea was violent,
The sea was cloudy,
The sea was fierce,
The sea was full of poems.

The sea was exciting,
The sea was cute,
The sea had roughness,
The sea had calmness,
Valentines on the romantic ocean sea.

Natalie Chikodzore (8)
Marycourt School

THE ATLANTIC

The calm sea is cold.
The calm sea is soft.
The calm sea is blue.
The calm sea is shiny.
The calm sea is relaxing.
The calm sea is gentle.
The calm sea is rippling.
The rough sea is fierce.
The rough sea is freezing.
The rough sea is noisy.
The rough sea is violent.
The rough sea is stormy.
The rough sea is curling.
The rough sea is windy

But now it's full of people.

Bianca Cleaver (8)
Marycourt School

I CAN...

I can see the sea,
I can hear the waves,
I can see the caves,
I can feel the spray,
I can see the children play,
I can see the yellow sand,
I can feel the sand rushing through my hand,
I can eat the ice creams,
I can taste the extremes,
I love the beach.

Deanna Orpin (8)
Marycourt School

THE SEA

The sea is smooth.
You can hear the gulls crying on the seashore.
When the sea is rough it is stormy
And when boats are out they rock side to side.

Sometimes the sea is velvety silver and shiny.
Sometimes people are relaxed in the sun
And are enjoying themselves.
At the sea it is very windy.
The waves crash into the beach very quickly.
The sea is blue and calming.

Caroline Brew (8)
Marycourt School

THE SEA

Calm
The sea is calm
It is in our palm
We think how wonderful it is
It is cold and smooth and silky

Rough
The waves blow together
Crashing us down
It will take us to a faraway land
Making sure it doesn't stop
Finally it calms down.

James Morgan (8)
Marycourt School

I DO THIS . . .

On Monday I sleep in my big bed loudly,
I swim in the blue water madly,
Monday is a boring day.

On Tuesday I snore in my small bed quietly,
I play outside with my football noisily,
Tuesday is a sunny day.

On Wednesday I go on my roller skates slowly,
I chew on my white bone quickly,
Wednesday is a fun day.

On Thursday I drink orange beer wildly,
I hop on my brown leg steadily,
Thursday is a funny day.

On Friday I blow my nose loudly,
I get out of my warm bed slowly,
Friday is a strange day.

On Saturday I speak in the cold room clearly,
I jump in the big pantomime crazily,
Saturday is a beautiful day.

On Sunday I go to the white dome slowly,
I ride my blue bike fast,
Sunday is a happy day.

Marco Netto (8)
Marycourt School

HORSES

Horses are brown, black and white,
Stable and field they like the most,
Oats and carrots they desire to chew,
Playtime is a game.
They canter around the long grassy fields,
Stay warm in the stubbly, thin hay,
Giving children horse rides on their fluffy backs,
What lovely creatures they are!

Claire Vine (9)
Marycourt School

MY HOBBY

F   un
O   utside
O   ffside
T   eam
B   all
A   ctive
L   eeds United
L   eagues

My hobby
Is football.

Sarah Rodwell (10)
Marycourt School

I Do This All Week

On Mondays
I get up from a warm bed sleepily
I run to mad Spain crazily
Monday is a sunny day.

On Tuesday
I drink brown beer madly
I chew my food on the table quickly
Tuesday is a fun day.

On Wednesday
I pick up small Marco quickly
I fall in the cold river scarily
Wednesday is a cool day.

On Thursday
I run to cargo house slowly
I throw the small ball high
Thursday is a calm day.

On Friday
I speak in class five scarily
I play in the park with William
Friday is a pretty day.

On Saturday
I run one hundred miles slowly
I go on my scooter happily
Saturday is a happy day.

On Sunday
I pick up my small hamster carefully
I take my cat to the vet sadly
Sunday is a sad day.

Declan Johnson (8)
Marycourt School

STORM

Leaves swirling,
Water floods whirling,
Winds howling,
The storm has started.

Trees tumbling,
Heating rumbling,
Everyone freezing,
And the storm goes on.

Dustbins clashing,
Lightning flashing,
Fences collapsing,
And still the storm goes on.

It's annoying,
It's frightening,
It's exciting,
But it still goes on.

Walls are trembling,
Twigs snapping,
Everything's wobbling,
The storm is now quieting.

Fences bending,
Windows defending,
At last it's ending,
The storms finally stopped.

Lisa Hancock (10)
North Baddesley County Junior School

THE MOON

If I lived on the moon,
I would be the only one,
So I wouldn't have to share my space room
And I might have to leave my dad and mum.

My brothers will be aliens,
So might my mum and dad,
If the wind blows my brothers away
We will all be really sad.

The wind, the storm and the blowing air,
Will blow the giant marquee,
Booms and flounders past you
Like a swan at sea.

Nuts and bulbs blowing away,
Right up in the air,
People trying to catch them,
Some people can't bear.

Lewis Down (10)
North Baddesley County Junior School

TRAPPED

I am trapped in my own little room,
But outside is the storm of doom,
I won't cry, I won't fret,
This storm will go back to where it was set.

But what if I cry, what if I fret,
Then it will still be here I bet,
I'll be scared stiff,
Like my dad in a cable car lift.

The rivers are rising, oh what shall I do,
It will be rushing into my house soon,
I think that there might
Be a typhoon.

David Clamp (9)
North Baddesley County Junior School

THE STORM

The rain drummed on the roof tiles,
The wind and mist whistled loud.
The sea sent ships turning,
Through dark and foggy cloud.

The waves and mist kept flowing,
Through grumpy and foggy skies.
A nightmare dream for sailors,
A sight for everyone's eyes.

To get to school, a nightmare,
Drenching you and me.
I wouldn't like to be a sailor,
Sailing on the sea.

Is the wind so mighty strong?
Ripping off the tiles.
Can it pick up you and me,
And turn buildings into piles?

The storm builds up power,
Panic! Thunder and lightning.
Fences smashed, windows blown in,
The sight is oh so frightening.

James Bullock (9)
North Baddesley County Junior School

THE SEA

The wind is howling against the boat
It tips to the side
The sea gathers all its strength
Nearly makes the boat commit suicide.

All the passengers wonder
What will happen next
How the boat will stay afloat
Until they dock so safe.

The captain says he will not go back
The company says 'yes'
All the lorries out there wonder
What they're in for.

But me and you know
That out on that sea
No one can survive
When it is this stormy.

David Goodwin (10)
North Baddesley County Junior School

FROSTY DAYS

I get cold and wet, frosty and blue,
As I skip through the sparkling snow,
The people play all through the day,
And build funny, fluffy snowmen.

The snow on the ground makes a squelchy sound
As the snow comes falling down
The people prance, sing and dance,
For it is Christmas Day!

Chelsea Hayward (8)
Rookesbury Park School

WINTER WARMTH

The season is winter, it's cold and bleak
There's nothing to do from week to week,
Except sit by the fire, crackling and hot
Sipping my cocoa, I like it a lot.

I like being snug and warm,
Even when there's a raging storm
I like mince pies when they're still hot
And Father Christmas, believe him or not.

I like pretty snowflakes, pure and clean,
Building snowmen, I hope they'll be seen.
But I really don't like the dark dull rain,
I can't wait till it's summer again!

Hannah Furby (8)
Rookesbury Park School

BAD BROOMS

B   eastly black hair,
R   ound beady eyes,
O   dious, mean and she is
O   bserving in everyone's conversations.
M   ischievously creeping around,
S   pells she'll cast upon you,
T   iny torn and jagged hat,
I   nsane with her clothes,
C   reatures crawl all over her.
K   neel down and obey her or
S   he'll cook you in her cauldron!

Allix Moore (9)
Rookesbury Park School

WICKED WITCHES

Witches all scowl,
Witches all howl,
In the depths of the night,
They'll give you a fright.

In her house,
She has a bat and a mouse.
But she keeps in her hat,
Her big fat cat.

Making spells,
With freaky smells.
On her broomstick she flies,
Out into the skies.

Fiona Findlater (8)
Rookesbury Park School

WINTER MONTHS

Cold and gloomy, damp and grey,
Chilly and damp and soggy the hay.
These describe November's weather,
Foggy, boggy, mould on the heather.

Icy, fresh, crisp as snow,
Temperature's dropping to make trees glow.
December's the month of much glee,
Tinsel and glitter, it's Christmas you see!

Jasmine Riggs-Bristow (7)
Rookesbury Park School

MONKEYS

He has furry hair.
His fur is as smooth as a horse.
His fingers are just like ours.
His eyes are as big as ever.
He stretched and stretched.

His teeth are spiky and long.
His tail is shimmering and shining.
He likes to hang from a branch,
Forever and ever upside down.

He likes to eat leaves and trees.
He sits on a branch eating a banana.
Monkeys are just like people.
They look like people, they smile like people,
Just like you and me!

Victoria Mathias-Jones (10)
Rookesbury Park School

DULL DAYS

Winter, winter, cold as ice,
Howling noises, they're not nice!
The snow is white as lightning,
I find the storms quite frightening!
I sit by the fire and read a book,
Then I go outside to have a look.
I notice that it's frosty and cold,
The robins are singing, they're so bold!

Sarah-Lucille Forfar (8)
Rookesbury Park School

MONKEYS

Their tails are like fur on a stick,
Their mouths are like opening caves,
The noise they make is like a door screeching.

They have fur which is all rumpled and spiky,
Their noses are like flat triangles,
They have brown bright eyes that shine,
And big ears that have not yet been cleaned.

They have hands almost like ours with fingers and nails,
And feet which are all dry and scaly,
Their skin is the colour of a crumpled peach
And they have kind looking faces.

Daisy White (9)
Rookesbury Park School

WINTER DAYS

It's dark in the morning,
When I get up,
And dark at night,
When I have my cup,
Of Ovaltine before I clean,
My teeth and go to bed.

It's cold in the mornings,
Freezing at night,
Winter's here for sure,
That's right,
It's nearly here, it's Christmastime,
Then spring is standing next in line.

Sophie White (7)
Rookesbury Park School

A SONNET FOR DAVID

Slowly trudging down the road,
On a journey to freedom he'd say,
Trudging along, trudging along,
With only a stop to lay.

They might come after him,
They being them,
The people that capture you while you're in your den,
'Will they capture me?' said he, 'Will they capture me?'

He runs like a bird on the wing they all say,
With a free will like never before,
Pausing only to eat and to pray,
Freedom is the prize he really wants.

He will have freedom one day,
Yes, he will have freedom one day.

Bryony Hayward (11)
Rookesbury Park School

THE WINTER WEEKS

Winter is so icy and bare,
And really, really cold.
But do you know what? I don't care.
Even when the wind takes hold,
Giving the animals a great big scare,
Apart from the fox, who is so bold
The footprints left belong to the hare
Who is waiting while spring's on hold.

Lauren Davis (8)
Rookesbury Park School

WICKED WITCHES

There is a witch,
All in black.
A wicked witch
With a pointed hat.
And an evil, spitting, nasty cat
Nasty spells, gruesome potions,
She'll get you in her power.

With a magic broomstick,
She flies in the night,
Her back is all bent,
Her toes all square,
Her nose is like a hook,
Her fingers scratch like claws.

Fiona Fairbairn (8)
Rookesbury Park School

SPRING'S ARRIVAL

Lambs frolic in the fields,
Discovering the green, lush grass.
Flowers peep from winter beds,
Like multicoloured paint.
Blossom takes over the trees stiffness,
Replacing it with bright colours.
Leaves grow on naked trees,
Filling their branches with life,
A reviving cloak of green.
Sunshine fills the land with warmth,
Spring has arrived!

Nicola Cartwright (11)
Rookesbury Park School

COMING HOME

Alone, frightened,
Scared, lonely.

Will she like me?
Will she recognise me?
Will she talk to me?
Will she remember me?
Will anyone like me?

I want to go Back Home.

Alone, frightened,
Scared, lonely.

Is this England?
Is this home?
Is this a friend?
Is this an enemy?
Is this my mum?

I want to go Back Home.

Clementine Turner-Powell (12)
Rookesbury Park School

WINTER

The trees are bare, with snow on the branches
The days get shorter,
The nights get longer,
It rains a lot.
When we get up it is misty,
In winter people don't want to get out of bed,
Some days are cold, icy, foggy,
In winter we can build snowmen.

Harriet Dunkason (7)
Rookesbury Park School

NARNIA AND THE WARDROBE

When Lucy went into the wardrobe
She didn't know what she would see
She thought it would just be hats and coats
But instead she saw some trees.

She turned around towards a bright light
And fir trees covered in snow
And then she realised she wasn't alone
As the winds began to blow.

A fawn come skipping down a path
Two horns upon his head,
On seeing Lucy he jumped in fright,
'Good gracious me,' he said.

Lucy shook his hand,
And asked him for his name
'My name is Tumnus' he replied
And looked rather ashamed.

'Would you like to come with me'
The little fawn quickly said,
'Yes please,' she replied with glee
So to his cave he led.

Katie Blunden
Rookesbury Park School

FINALLY FREE

A boy was walking round and round,
When he heard a quiet sound.
A man was standing by his side,
And told the boy to run away.

Then the boy did as he was told,
He wasn't more than ten years old.
Then he travelled for months on end
Till he reached his destination.

Svetlana Kotova (11)
Rookesbury Park School

ALONE

Standing alone,
So lost and forlorn,
He whimpers a moan,
His feet tired and worn.

A boy so young
He's friendless for sure,
The burning hot sun
Making his back sore.

He looks so strange,
His eyes are silent,
They never change,
They're never violent.

He's learning trust,
That most men are kind,
He knows he must
Carry on and find

A family,
Who he'll care for,
Live happily,
He will roam no more!

Stephanie Melvin (10)
Rookesbury Park School

The Most Beautiful Season

Whenever spring is coming
You'll never know she's there,
Until you look out your window
And the sun suddenly comes near.

The birds are tweeting sweetly,
Higher and higher they fly,
Until they almost reach the sun,
You keep trying to ask them why.

The flowers bloom with beauty,
Stretching as far as they can,
Down looks the tree with sympathy
As she's much taller as she stands.

This is part of spring's beauty,
Out of the seasons she's the best,
She is by far the prettiest,
So much better than the rest.

Majiri Otobo (12)
Rookesbury Park School

Wicked Witches

Witches are horrible and ugly,
They live in terrifying houses
And look evil and tatty.
When carrying a little black cat
Their faces look evil
And noses are ugly,
Suddenly the lights go dark
Then all the witches come out!

Antonia Sugden (8)
Rookesbury Park School

NARNIA

It's always cold in Narnia,
The land that's always white,
Lucy's feet among the snow,
Heading for the light.

Branches scratching on her face,
The forest dark and damp,
In the mist she sees
A little yellow lamp.

The lamp that lights the way ahead,
The lamp that lights the path,
Taking her onward through the dark
Home to her warm hearth.

Elena Preston-Davis (8)
Rookesbury Park School

DOLPHINS

Their skin is as smooth as silk.
Their cry is like a siren.
They are quick unlike an old granny.
They are as sweet as a sleeping baby.
They move as gracefully as a ballerina
And dance through the water.
They are as lively as a little child.
When you see them you want to stroke them.
It has been said they are as intelligent as man.
Dolphins.

Camilla Culshaw (10)
Rookesbury Park School

STORM

His eyes are like a pool of warm chocolate,
Which shimmer in the moonlight,
His chestnut silk coat shining like a newly fallen conker,
Which came from a great tree.

His white flash across his flank is like a lightning streak,
Which has come from a great storm,
His ears are like pointed radars,
Which swivel at the slightest sound.

His hooves beat the ground like an African drum,
As he pounds the solid earth,
His tail streams like a flag in the wind,
As he flies across the horizon.

Stephanie Dampney (10)
Rookesbury Park School

RACING PIGEON

Pigeons preen and peck
Waiting for the next race day,
Flying round and round to practise,
Ducking and taking off together
Waiting for the next race day.

When race day comes they are transported away
To far and foreign lands,
They are let go, they sprint all day long,
When hungry they will not stop.
They fly home exhausted to their tin of pigeon food.

Sophie Brown (11)
Rookesbury Park School

DOLPHINS

Dolphins rushing through the sea,
Speeding home rapidly for their tea,
Gliding swiftly through the water,
Diamond droplets shimmer in the heat.

Capturing their prey,
Prickly ones and slimy ones,
Sickly ones and shiny ones.

Leaping, bounding through the clear salty surf,
Their light blue skin glistens,
Racing towards the setting sun,
Their day is over, they drift, drift, drift,
As quiet and contented as can be.

Laura Parker (9)
Rookesbury Park School

MY DOG SAM

My dog has eyes like stars in the sky,
When he looks at me he really wants food or love.
His ears are like cotton wool, but he still hears well.
In the car his ears flap in the breeze.
His teeth are like hard rock, but he doesn't bite hard.
His tail is as soft as slippers, I like to touch it.
His nose is like wet raindrop, but it can be a hot stove.
His claws are like a sharp blade, if he scratches me it hurts
His whiskers are thin and tickle,
His body is really soft and shiny.
I don't care what he looks like
Because I love him the way he is!

Gilly Windebank (11)
Rookesbury Park School

DIZZY THE PONY

Her eyes are a deep blue sea,
Lashing out at people who come too near,

Fur soft as marshmallows,

Neigh like a distant rumble of thunder
Slowly getting nearer,

Her hooves hard as a brick wall,

Teeth blunt as stalks of bananas,

Muzzle soft as a feather cushion,

Her forelock, tail and mane like
Untangled hay.

Olivia Galloway (10)
Rookesbury Park School

THE LION'S DAY

A lazy lion, shakes his powerful mane and yawns,
Showing his fatal, deadly teeth.
A lioness brings her prey and drops it by him.
Staring at him lays a dead zebra,
He tears the meat gently, the lioness sleeps.
Hyenas are giggling in the distance,
Vultures are circling high above,
He closes his eyes and goes to sleep.
His golden brown coat blazes in the sun.

Elo Otobo (9)
Rookesbury Park School

FREE FROM CAPTIVITY

Terrible torture, the hunger and pain
Those fearful feelings no longer remain
Freedom is hopefully mine at last
Days spent in darkness are now in the past.

I have never seen such sights before
Green hills, open moors, the sparkling seashore
Swooping seagulls, fine fragrant flowers
Tall trees standing up like towers.

The warmth of the shimmering sunshine
All this breathtaking beauty is mine
A bright future is now ahead of me
Oh how wonderful it is to be free!

Lauren Burton (10)
Rookesbury Park School

THE NEVER-ENDING JOURNEY

Slowly, calmly, I did travel,
Down the dark, cold road I fled.
I am starting to unravel
Every step with care I tread.

As scary faces glare and stare
Who to trust, to keep me safe?
All alone, no one to care,
All I am is a scruffy waif.

Trotting along on the gravel,
All I want is to be fed,
I must now start my travel,
I must now use all of my head.

Laura Wagstaff (11)
Rookesbury Park School

WHAT SHALL I DO?

Should I ask the man for a lift?
To help him choose should I give him a gift?
All I have to give is bread
If he says 'more' to Denmark I'll tread.

I could give my water in a flask,
But that would be a very hard task!
What am I putting into my head?
I shall only give him my piece of bread.

Lucky for me the man was kind,
Perugia for me he would find.
He smiled and gave me lots of bread
But, talked until it hurt my head.

Charlotte Boardman (10)
Rookesbury Park School

MY ANGEL OF COURAGE

I've always been afraid of someone,
Never wanting to be alone.
But she has always cared for me,
My angel of courage, with me she's flown.

I've asked her for her own opinion,
Each time I'm in despair,
Sometimes it is my heart that breaks,
But she is always there.

My courage grows each time she smiles,
Each time I see her star.
She's the one who'll carry me through
My journeys near and far.

Laetitia Clarke (10)
Rookesbury Park School

THE COLOURS OF THE RAINBOW

Orange, blue, purple and green,
All these colours I have seen,
Red and pink and lilac too,
A bunch of roses given to you.

Yellow, silver, bronze and gold,
Shimmering colours bright and bold,
Colours here to set me free,
With strokes and flashes for you to see.

All the colours I have seen,
The blue of oceans and brown of beans,
All the colours of the world,
The leaves curled up and fall down unfurled.

Tilly Wheating (10)
Rookesbury Park School

THE FIRE BIRD

As the bird flaps her wings ready to fly,
Her feathers break off and say goodbye.
The bird stands naked in the cold,
Her feathers departed, bright and gold.

Scattered feathers swirling free,
The beautiful bird no longer to be.
Just her naked body there,
Lonely, abandoned, totally bare.

There she stays until that day,
When warmth and sunshine break the way.
And tiny feathers start to grow,
Our beautiful bird will be ready for show.

Tara Wheating (12)
Rookesbury Park School

THERE'S A WITCH

There's a witch
All in black
With a pointed nose
And a crooked hat.
She has a broomstick
And a black cape,
Her fingers are claws
Her toes a funny shape.
She runs and has a take-off
And up she flies,
Cackling, her grey hair streaming
As she shoots through the skies.
Landing by a cottage,
A crumbling little house,
She climbs through the window,
Creeping like a mouse.
She switches on the light,
To turn her house bright
You can see her shadow
Dancing with the night.
She takes her skeleton pot
And throws in things like these:
Spider's legs, worm's tails,
Newt's eyes and mouldy cheese.
She mixes them together,
What a sight to see!
Who would like to drink that potion?
Certainly not me!

Alice Pollock (9)
Rookesbury Park School

FEELING OUT

When I first came here
England was strange to me,
Language was different to me,
Everything was different to me,
But now I've got used to it.

When I first went to the dining room,
Everyone was staring at me,
I felt very scared,
But now I've got used to it.

When I first went to the boarding house
Everyone was looking at me,
Everything was different to me,
But now I've got used to it.

Queenie Lin Qing Qing (11)
Rookesbury Park School

POTIONS AND SPELLS

P   iercing eyes, horribly wise
O   dious cat, pointed hat.
T   errifying smile, gruesome guile
I   ngredients vile, her spells to compile
O   n her broomstick she flies
N   ight cloaks her disguise
S   earching for frog, newt and toad.

S   creams and moans, grinding bones
P   archment old, spells untold,
E   vil cackle, fires crackle
L   eaning over her cauldron
L   unging, in she falls!

Caroline Butten (9)
Rookesbury Park School

MY SWEET AND SOFT SPRING

Spring is beautiful as can be,
The flowers came out just for me.
Lots of blossoms full of bloom,
Already forgotten, winter's gloom.

The heat of the burning hot sun,
Looks like a yellow bright sky bun.
It has slowly warmed my golden skin,
It smiles on me, with a great big grin.

The high trees stand, full of flowers,
A painted picture, stare for hours.
The whistling wind makes me blind,
Spring can be so cruel, yet kind.

Aleshia Fung (11)
Rookesbury Park School

THE BEAUTIFUL SEASON

In spring little animals are born,
Cute as can be, large or small.
They learn how to walk
And spring and jump
And catch their prey
In the month of May.
Then they grow up
And take things in, day by day.
Spring is here
And it is clear
It won't stay forever.
Spring is very, very clever.

Charlotte Gill (11)
Rookesbury Park School

SCENES OF SPRING

Dewdrops glisten in the grass,
Like diamonds scattered on velvet.
Silky cobwebs are like necklaces,
Strung with precious gems and minerals.

April showers sparkle,
Like glitter from a pot.
New leaves are like ballerinas
Springing into a hop.

Snowdrops shimmer white
In the morning light.
Daffodils stand boldly,
Yellow in the sun.

Rainbows reaching into the sky
Like a paint palette.

Hannah Whittle (11)
Rookesbury Park School

JOURNEY

J   oyful life and then
O   ur loved ones die,
U   pset, we cry,
R   ising sun,
N   ow young ones grow,
E   lderly, you're weak,
Y   our life ends . . .

Sophie Bourke (10)
St Mary's RC Primary School, Gosport

LIFE

Life is a baby being born into the world.
Life is someone dying every second.
Life is someone travelling over the azure sea.
Life is someone making fun of a fat person.
Life is a fresh apple falling to the ground.
Life is a friend never betraying you.
Life is a glass falling out of a shaking hand.
Life is a heart being broken every day.
Life is what a human has.
Life is love.
Life is a mystery.

But life is not just all of these things,
It's something that you want it to be,
But sometimes it's emptiness in someone's life.

So life is up to you!

Chelsea Ferrol (10)
St Mary's RC Primary School, Gosport

TAKE OFF TO ST LUCIA

Engine's shake
People sleep
Plane moves
My heart leaps.

Heart quivering
I tire
Clenching seat
Hope no fire.

We're at the end
Babies cry
Bodies shaking
So am I!

People awakening
People shouting
Almost there
No doubting.

Sarah Kelly (9)
St Mary's RC Primary School, Gosport

TRAVEL

At home alone
I sat on my own
Thinking that something was there

So I went for walk
But I heard a squawk
But still nothing was there

I went to the wood
And tripped over some goods
I thought that a pirate lived there

I came out of the woods
Along with my goods
And then made my journey home

At home at last
My travel has past
I think I will go to my bed.

Skye Hall (10)
St Mary's RC Primary School, Gosport

TRAVELLING

Car, bus, taxi,
To travel.
Aeroplane,
To travel.
Boat and ferry,
To travel,
To travel.

In the dark,
To travel.
In the light,
To travel.
All day long,
To travel,
To travel.

Over sea,
To travel.
Over land,
To travel.
Over fluffy clouds,
To travel,
To travel.

Rachel Landon (10)
St Mary's RC Primary School, Gosport

THE OCEAN

The azure water rippled

Afar you hear a melancholy cry,
Swooping and swaying, were wretched seagulls,
Trying to catch a bite to eat,
Tropical fishes swim to and fro,
Beneath the azure rippled water.

On a cautious rock at the edge of the world,
You hear a pleading cry,
A song by the lonely, lost mermaid,
She has wished for true love.

The message is sent from the lonely,
Lost mermaid,
For she, the mermaid with long,
Undulating, green hair,
Was waiting for a life saving answer.

The sun trickled down on her luminous face,
But there was no news,
Meanwhile her answer had not come,
She tempted a sailor with her luxurious melody.

Days passed,
Nights travelled.

Jane Swords (10)
St Mary's RC Primary School, Gosport

IMAGINE

Imagine walking on the perpetual moon,
Imagine starring in a cartoon.

Imagine a raging storm,
Imagine a never-ending story.

Imagine petting a wealthy cat,
Imagine being silly Postman Pat.

Imagine talking to a walking tree,
Imagine having your favourite tea.

Imagine having beautiful wings,
Imagine wearing nine gold rings.

Imagine walking on the perpetual moon,
Imagine starring in a cartoon.

Just imagine.

Kathleen Smith (10)
St Mary's RC Primary School, Gosport

TAKE-OFF

I'm scared
Heart beats
Plane moves
A few feet.

Travelling high
Travelling low
Day and night
What a blow.

Planes ride
In the air
Stay alive
Nearly there.

Plane stops
With a bang
Heart fails
Birds sang.

Samantha Fairclough (10)
St Mary's RC Primary School, Gosport

THE STORM

The howling of the trees,
The blast of thunder vandalising the cities,
Lightning hitting trees . . . silence.
Thunder crashing down hitting streams,
Crushing statues into tiny smithereens,
. . . silence, silence.

Jacob Wilson (11)
St Patrick's Catholic Primary School, Woolston

THE STORM

The violent wind as hard as a hurricane,
Rough trees thrashing wildly from side to side,
Blustery clouds split apart so the sparkling
Stars sprinkle down,
The outbreaking thundery storm smashes down
Bins and blows litter around.

Kirsty Lee (11)
St Patrick's Catholic Primary School, Woolston

SPACE

I look up at the whirling, spinning vortex
Which is space, I watch the stars
Blowing holes in the black velvet.
Those white dots look as though they have
Been sewn into the sky. The darkness
Being pierced by the gas of the stars,
This is space.

Cameron Hall (11)
St Patrick's Catholic Primary School, Woolston

WEATHER

Wind viciously beating the weathered branches,
Torrential rain lashing the windowpane like a cat of nine tails,
A fork of lightning illuminating the sky,
Wind picking up everything in its path,
Then hitting the ground like the patter of a million tiny feet.

Amy Stokes (11)
St Patrick's Catholic Primary School, Woolston

STARS

Huge glowing basketballs thrown into the pitch-black sky,
Glitter strung all over the galaxy like Christmas tree lights,
Bright shiny stars sown like glowing seeds on a black field,
Stars floating in infinity like a hovercraft.

Christopher Lee (11)
St Patrick's Catholic Primary School, Woolston

FIREWORKS

A thick quilt of rich black silk
Sprinkles of luminous sequins and jewels.
Fireworks - screaming and screeching like a strangled cat.
Twisting and revolving like a bony hand
Turning a wooden ladle.
Illuminated sparks - elegant but devious
Paint pictures in the deep, dark sky,
Endless fun.
Catherine wheels spinning around,
Colours colliding with each other.
A raging fire melts away into the sky,
Wood crackling like a witch's snigger.

Caroline Misselbrook (11)
St Patrick's Catholic Primary School, Woolston

FIREWORKS

Exploding light in the black satin sky,
Catherine wheels swirling and spinning
Like a park roundabout, rockets whiz,
Whoosh! Boom! Red, yellow, green lights everywhere,
People stunned while the deep red and orange,
Fire blazing like the sun on a hot sunny day,
The smell of hot dogs and burgers in the air
Boom! Boom!
More fireworks exploding, then
It's all over, people still laughing.

Ellen Mooney (11)
St Patrick's Catholic Primary School, Woolston

BONFIRE NIGHT

The sky black as a piece of velvet,
Darker and deeper than a black hole,
Stars glittering and gleaming like a thousand
Jewels over a black banner,
A bonfire crackling, fizzing like a huge
Mass of flames, a huge shining sun.
Vicious little sparkler nipping at my hand,
Golden sparks falling to the ground,
Rockets jumping and whistling then exploding
Into a million pieces,
Sizzling burgers giving a smell of cooked meat,
Salad, ready to be put into burgers,
Resting on the barbecue.
Sun coming up: The 6th of November.

Jeanne-Irène Zimmermann (11)
St Patrick's Catholic Primary School, Woolston

AT SEA

Waves splashing the side
A carpet of blue
The wind in the sail
Sea life coming up to get a closer look.

The speed and the thrill
Sailing far the busy land
The weather is hot
The sun a violent orange.

Leo Jack (11)
St Patrick's Catholic Primary School, Woolston

THUNDER AND LIGHTNING

The evil torrential
Rain blasting against
The pavement.

Twisting like a tornado
Round the train,
As if it has its own brain.

The lightning hammering
Against the heavy grey clouds,
Chasing after it comes
The disturbing eardrum noise.
Thunder!

Yasmin Kitchen (11)
St Patrick's Catholic Primary School, Woolston

BONFIRE NIGHT

Fireworks exploding from corner to corner,
Rockets flying from the sky to the ground,
Then a sudden bang, bang, bang
And followed by a Catherine wheel spinning
Around and around.
But now as slow as a merry-go-round,
The sparklers spitting all over the place
And also pinching and burning
The top of my face.

Emily Whitmarsh (11)
St Patrick's Catholic Primary School, Woolston

THE STORM

The trees look like they are quivering,
Howls of the blustery monsoon wind echoes the street,
The torrential flooding thunderously crashes
Against the road and path like the sparks from
A steam train scattering across the surface.
The thunder and lightning join forces and buries
Into the ground like a racing car blistering on
The track and crashing into a barrier,
Bang, smack, explosion, the car's batter into the lamp posts.
Finally the grey clouds part from each other and
The moon's dazzling shine can be seen again.

Connor Barnett (11)
St Patrick's Catholic Primary School, Woolston

BONFIRE AND FIREWORK NIGHT

Raindrops fill the eerie sky,
While rushing down from the sky,
While shooting stars shoot up again,
Screaming aloud the massive crowd.

The Catherine wheel spinning around
Just as fast as waltzers,
The bonfire raging like the gleaming sun.

Chelsea Helliwell (11)
St Patrick's Catholic Primary School, Woolston

THE STORM

Smack, bang the thunder rang
The cruel crack as the lightning whacked,
Rain thrashed down like golf balls,
A vicious fire spreads through the woods,
Fire-fighters battle the powerful fire,
The night's floods swamp the battered landscape,
Animals unable to fight the strength of the storm,
Twisters getting ready to form,
To saturate everything below.

Joe Cameron (10)
St Patrick's Catholic Primary School, Woolston

THE WINNER'S CUP

I mounted the horse
I kicked with great force,
With a powerful buck, we went over the jump
And landed in a muffled thump,
Here we go, my horse was fed up,
So away with the winners in this years cup,
Dressage and jumping were a disaster,
They were mysteries I couldn't master,
Slowly, slowly, I dismounted,
Four faults and only the canter counted.

Lauren Bradley (11)
St Patrick's Catholic Primary School, Woolston

THE GALE

The wind is fierce
The town is wrecked
Lids of bins flying about
Like flying saucers
Trees falling one after another
The wind like wolves
Howling at the midnight moon.

Cars are shaking,
Like rattlesnakes,
Birds fighting against the winds,
Being pushed back,
Planes proving their strength,
Against the forceful winds,
People being swooped off their feet,
At the mercy of the winds.

Oliver Precious (11)
St Patrick's Catholic Primary School, Woolston

THE CAULDRON

It had been incredibly beastly,
The gate was torn off its frame,
Lids had been whisked all over the park,
Slates had been blasted off garage roofs.
The blare of a trumpeting wind responded
Like wolves howling.
A full moon attended throughout the misty clouds,
Which had swirled past,
As it boiled in the cauldron.

Brydie Upwood (11)
St Patrick's Catholic Primary School, Woolston

THE KILLER WORMS

The killer worms are coming
They're coming up your street
They're coming with an army
Which are hard to defeat.

They're teaming up with red ants
And with bumblebees too
They're all on one mission
And that's to kill you!

They just came up your staircase
They are now in your bedroom
I'm sure they'll grant you one thing
They'll grant you your doom.

It's lucky you are at work
So your lizard will scare them away
They'll run and run, but not for fun
Until the end of the day.

They jumped into your computer
And set up their own game
But the game was so boring
They killed themselves in shame.

So if your computer gets a bug
It isn't suffering from flu
It's the killer worms getting revenge
They are getting revenge on *you.*

Hugo Lewkowicz (10)
Sherborne House School

THE SUGAR PLUM CATERPILLAR

When I buy my weekly sweets from the local store
One day later when they have gone
I have to buy some more.
I wonder who is doing this, is it my brother Lee?
All I know for definite it certainly is not me.
I've found holes in my window, holes in my wall, holes in the heater,
They're really very small.
Whatever it is it must be a bug, spider or rat,
Cos now the house is falling down just because of that.
Now we are moving house I am really very glad
Cos Mum is going absolutely stark raving mad!

It's 20 years later now, I've passed all my exams,
I've turned into a pop star and got one million fans.
I read in a book one day and this is what I read,
That they found a little white caterpillar with a sugar plum head.
As I read more I realised and said
'Gotcha Sugar Thief,' now it was clear in my head.

Lucy Caldwell (10)
Sherborne House School

THE DAY MY MUM BECAME A CHICKEN

When my mum became a chicken
Was a very strange day indeed
For breakfast - no more cornflakes
But a great big bowl of seed!

I started to get worried
When she stood upon one leg
And began to make a clucking sound
And promptly laid an egg!

A crack appeared upon the egg
And then a bigger one
Until the egg was fully hatched
And out came a mini mum!

Hannah Chew (9)
Sherborne House School

MY FAMILY

My Dad

Dashing
Smashing

With it
Nit-wit

Artistic
Optimistic

Cheerful
Beer-full

Me

Loud
Proud

With it
Fidgit

Tall
Cool

Impetuous
Goddess

My Mum

Appealing
Endearing

With it
Exquisite

Lovely
Bubbly

Soothing
Approving

My brother

Happy
Chappie

With it
Midget

Sunny
Funny

Full of beans
Won't eat his greens!

Eleanor Taylor (9)
Sherborne House School

THE ELEPHANT WHO SNORES

One day I went to the zoo,
And what do you think I saw?
An elephant fast asleep,
With such an enormous snore.

He shared a bed with his brother,
And always had the top bunk,
And dangling over the edge,
Was a noisy, long, grey trunk!

His brother woke up with a fright,
And up from his bed he rose,
And deciding to fix his unsociable brother,
Stuffed a melon right up his nose.

Felicity de Vere (9)
Sherborne House School

THE TOILET MONSTER

I sat on the toilet one day
And I heard a voice growl 'Hey!'
I got such a scare
I could not bare
The creature standing there

He was greeny brown
And wore a frown
It wasn't a very nice sight

I stood there . . . still,
It was such a thrill
I couldn't sleep all night.

Sophie Livesey (9)
Sherborne House School

No Way!

I went home needing my mum for a favour
So when I got there I was on my best behaviour
On my way I bought my mum some smellies
Chocolates, mints, sherbet and jellies.
I gave them to her she said she liked them a lot
I sensed some suspicion on what was my plot.
How could I say it? What could I do?
I tried but it came out 'Can I please go to the loo!'
Back to my problem, what to do now?
I knew what I wanted but couldn't say how.
It was only a disco, why was it wrong?
I'd come back at twelve but she'd say it's too long.
I plucked up my courage to finally ask
My mother's features were set like a mask.
She took a deep breath what would she say?
Then just what I dreaded it came,
'No way!'

Alexandra Hagger (10)
Sherborne House School

I Like To Sit Upon This Hill

I like to sit upon this hill
And watch the sun go down,
To see the reds and the golds come out of the folds in the sun.
I like to sit upon this hill
And watch the stars come up,
To see them winking at me brighter and brighter.
I like to lie upon this hill,
And see the night sky,
To feel the grass and leaves covering me,
And to know how lucky I am.

Helena Wealleans (10)
Sherborne House School

SKIING, SKIING, SKIING!

Skiing, skiing, skiing, this is the sport for me!
Whizzing down the mountainside, happy as can be

To the chairlift up I go
To the top of the mountain, lots of snow

What's that up in front of me
Is it a yeti, can it be?

Or is it a monster
To make me jump?

Ha ha . . . it's my dad all covered in snow
He is smothered from head to toe!

'Watch out Jenny!' I hear him say
Too late, I was looking the other way!

Head first bang into a tree,
Now it's me looking like a yeti!

Skiing is sporty, skiing is fun
It's one hundred times faster than going for a run!

Jenny Cotton (9)
Sherborne House School

SARAH

I once knew a girl named Sarah,
And I found it very difficult to bear her.
Oh how I wish she'd go away,
But instead my mum said she could come to stay.
So I complained to my dad (who was drinking his beer)
'Come on Dad, don't let her stay here!'
Dad said, 'Let her stay a night at least.
She's not a horrible beast.'

So I went upstairs saying I didn't care,
But when she came,
We played a game
With my teddy bear.
We now are each other's friends
So this is . . . The End.

Devika Pandit (9)
Sherborne House School

WHEN CHEESE TOOK OVER THE WORLD

Sarah was eating her lovely cheese roll,
When the cheese jumped out into her bowl
It started to grow hands, arms and legs,
When it laughed it startled even the eggs.

It laughed 'I am President Parmesan,'
Cheese came out of fridges and away they ran
Cheese took over everyone, even the Queen,
All was bad, the Cheeses were horrible and mean.

They ruled the land for seventeen years,
But one time when the Cheese had too many beers
They started to fight over who was best,
Everyone thought they were better than the rest.

Captain Cheddar said 'Swiss has too many holes,'
Swiss said 'Parmesan is a lump of coal!'
Then a great war broke out among the Cheese,
Sergeant Stilton fought in the war with ease.

But suddenly a mouse came to their war,
It ate them all until there were no more
As Swiss was swallowed, he let out a cry,
'One day Cheese will be back, we never die!'

Rosalind Sadowski (10)
Sherborne House School

ROCKERS

There are some old pensioners
Who moved next door
The strange thing is
They put down a dance floor!

With them they brought
A huge hi-fi system
And so many CDs
I just can't list them!

Isn't it strange, old pensioners
With a hi-fi system,
And so many CDs
That you just can't list them!

I've done some spying
I've worked it out
I know what this music stuff
Is all about.

They're what you call Rockers
And they wear leather things
And boy, oh boy
You should see them swing!

Victoria Hill (10)
Sherborne House School

SMOKEY AND CHARLIE

Smokey, Smokey, little cat
How I wonder why you're fat
Is it all your fluffy hair
Or because you're full of air
Smokey, Smokey, little cat
I think it's wind that makes you fat.

Charlie, Charlie, dog so big
I know your secret, you wear a wig
Don't you think you've got me fooled
Underneath I know you're bald
Charlie, Charlie, dog so big
Great idea mate, keep the wig.

Robyn Cadde (10)
Sherborne House School

THE HUNGRY CHIP

The hungry chip
Was having a heavenly sip
Of diet Coke
And went for a soak
And that's no joke!

The hungry chip
Was eating a lovely bowl of chocolate whip
Along came a fly
And passed him by
But he fell on a large custard pie.

The hungry chip
Whose name was 'Pip'
Went for a row on the lake
Whilst eating a delicious strawberry cake
And fell in the water, for goodness sake!

The hungry chip
Went to the local tip
To see what he could find to eat
All he could find was some rotting meat
So he trudged all the way home on weary feet.

Sarah Crampton-Barden (9)
Sherborne House School

THE GOBLIN IN MY WARDROBE

One day I opened my wardrobe
and got a terrible fright!
For there I saw a
great big, slimy, green goblin

It stood there, staring at me with its
tennis ball-sized, yellow eyes.
It had sticking-out ears and birdlike feet,
Wrinkled skin and a pointy, long nose.
It was the ugliest thing I had ever seen.

At first I froze . . .
Then I screamed.

On hearing my cries my mum came running,
'Whatever's the matter?' she screeched.
We opened the wardrobe door, but
the goblin had gone!

'It's only your school uniform fallen on the floor!'

Joanna Tung (10)
Sherborne House School

SPRING

In spring, when flowers blossom
And baby lambs are born
The cuckoo sings its joyful song
Yet I wonder why this season
Is so beautiful
Maybe it's God's favourite season
It's definitely mine.

William Francis (8)
Sherborne House School

THE GROOVY CHICK

I have a chick called Groovy
And she likes to groove all night
At night you should see the sight
In her dress
And it's a mess
But there's something I must tell you
A secret I should share
Because it's not what she looks like that matters
As her personality is crackers!

I have a chick called Groovy
And she likes to groove all night
Sometimes she really gives me a fright
I have to watch out that she doesn't bite
But there's something I should tell you
A secret I should share
Because it's not what she looks like that matters
As her personality is crackers!

I have a chick called Groovy
And she likes to groove all night
She has lots of friends that love her
And soft fluffy fur
But there's something I should tell you
A secret I must share
Because it's not what she looks like that matters
As she is fluffy, flitty and full of flair.

Ellie Stiles (9)
Sherborne House School

THE AMAZING CAKE

I once baked a cake that could talk, swim, run and walk,
His eyes were Smarties with little dots on top,
His nose was made out of Jelly Tots,
His teeth and lips were made out of gums,
But the cake did not have any fingers or thumbs.

'Come on,' I said, 'we're going out, Spongy.
When I look at you, you make me feel so hungry.'
When we went, he put on his hat,
Which was made out of this and that
Icing, hundreds and thousands, chocolate flakes,
Then we went to meet his mates.

'Hi Gingerbread Man, Peppermint Cake, how are you doing today?
This is a really good party, come on let's dance and play.'
Watching him dance, he looked so yummy,
All I could think of was him in my tummy,
Licking my lips, that was scrummy!

Isobel Stainton (10)
Sherborne House School

I'D RATHER BE . . .

I'd rather be a hammer than a nail,
I'd rather be a hawk than a snail,
I'd rather be a boat than a sail,
I'd rather be the postman than the mail.

I'd rather be a house than the floor,
I'd rather be at peace than at war,
I'd rather be the beach than the shore,
I'd rather be an apple than the core.

I'd rather be the wind than the rain,
I'd rather be in Thailand than in Spain,
I'd rather be in Rome than in Maine,
I'd rather be a rocket than a plane.

I'd rather be an ocean than a sea,
I'd rather be a door than a key,
I'd rather be a wood than a tree,
I'd rather be nobody else but me!

Serena Flavell (9)
Sherborne House School

WILL I EVER GET TO EAT MY CHOCOLATE?

As I opened my wrapper and peered inside
I could almost taste the chocolate.

It looked so delicious and creamy and sweet
And I was so hungry, so I couldn't wait any longer!

I raised it to my lips and was about to take a bite
When suddenly . . . the doorbell rang.

So I answered the door and much to my disgust
It was a man selling double glazing.

Please no! I don't want any double glazing. Leave me alone!
But he didn't. He carried on for half an hour.

'Right!' I said and went into the kitchen to get my chocolate,
But it had gone! I looked everywhere.

Disaster! The dog had eaten it.

Connie Harrison (11)
Sherborne House School

MAGIC WORLD

When I was young, one night I looked and saw a shooting star
It pointed to a magic world that seemed so very far
A fairy's wand, the moon so bright, a dragon, knight and king
A castle tall, a mountain blue, a brand new song to sing.

A candle burning, a shining light, the whistle in the breeze
The birds singing so beautifully, high up in the trees
A beach I go to in my dreams, the castle in my bed
If problems start to get me down I think of these instead.

My magic world is real enough, however strange it seems
I have often travelled there, a journey in my dreams
A desert there beneath the stars, a city in the sand
The ocean wide beyond the coast, a light to mark the land.

A rainbow high up in the sky, a pot of gold below
The sunlight and the gentle rain that makes the flowers grow
My magic land is near and far, wherever it may seem
You can always go there too if you can dream a dream.

Charlotte Oldam (9)
Sherborne House School

THE TRUTH ABOUT TEACHERS

The truth about teachers
Is not what you expect
They just aren't humans
They want your books perfect!

The truth about teachers
Is extremely scary
They slump in the staffroom
And drink coffee or tea!

The truth about teachers
Is they're really hard to please
And when you're in the lunch hall
They say 'Eat up your peas!'

The truth about teachers
Is just not what you expect
They really can't be human
Cause I'm always their suspect!

Holly Robson (10)
Sherborne House School

MOVING HOUSE

We went house-hunting and found a place,
Talked with estate agents about the price,
Worried about the house for a very long time,
Then told the bank and solicitor to get our papers in line,
Curtains were chosen and the removal men phoned,
After what seemed like ages we finally moved home.

When it comes to moving house, this is what I say:
The removal men worked hard but drank coffee all day,
Moving house is a grouch,
Can't put my feet up on the couch,
With boxes, boxes everywhere, I have no time to sit and stare . . .
At the TV - it's not connected!
This makes me feel so dejected.

You can't eat because there's no plates,
There's no sleep with the beds in such a state,
But apart from all this, moving house
Is just *great!*

John Dawes (10)
Sherborne House School

THE ENCHANTED PENCIL

Tommy took out his pencil
And then he started to write.
Before he had barely finished,
His pencil began to fight.

The pencil jumped down from the desk
And crawled underneath the chair.
It lifted Tommy right off the ground
And shouted 'Let's go to the fair!'

The pencil ran out of the door
And across the playground fast.
The park, the church, the clock shop
Were some of the things it passed.

When the pencil reached the fair,
It jumped on the carousel.
But when it tried to get off,
It accidentally fell.

A little boy picked it up,
He was Tommy's very best friend.
He brought it into school the next day
And gave it back to him in the end.

Alice Patterson (10)
Sherborne House School

MATTHEW

Matthew is very boring,
He is always loudly snoring.
He falls asleep so quick,
That he needs a hard kick
In order to open his book
And give it a good look.

Outside with a ball,
He is no good at all.
He does not know how to catch.
He will never be in a match.
If there was a medal for sleeping,
It would be his for keeping.

George Bliss (8)
Sherborne House School

THE KING WITH A BIG NOSE

King Arthur had the biggest nose
That ever had been seen.
He was married to the dearest lady,
The ugliest ever queen.

At breakfast time he ate and ate
Off the most enormous plate.
Unfortunately it was his nose
That knocked his plate onto his toes.

His wife the queen gave out a cry
And looked at all the messy pie.
'We'll have to get the Hoover in!'
She said with an enormous grin.

The mess was cleared, his plate renewed
King Arthur stared upon his food.
'Listen nose, you keep away!
Or else there'll be a price to pay!'

Although the day had just begun,
The morning had been full of fun!
What was to come had not yet been,
For King Arthur and his ugly queen!

Lois Power (11)
Sherborne House School

THE DAY ROBYN TURNED INTO A FROG

The day Robyn turned into a frog
Was a very sad day
Because Robyn was my best friend
And now, I don't have anyone to come and play.

One sunny day in May
Turned into an even sadder day
Because Robyn turned into a horse
And all she could do was neigh.

Then one day, Robyn lay down in the hay
'I like being a horse,' she started to say
'I don't know what's going to happen
But I hope I can stay.'

Philippa Bradbury (9)
Sherborne House School

EMILY

I knew a girl called Emily,
Who was very bright.
She read me a poem
About monsters in the night.
When she read it to me
It gave me a fright,
I enjoyed it when she read it
She read it from a height.
She found out after that
It was her Dad.
She told him off
For being very bad.

Ella Salkeld (8)
Sherborne House School

THE TOILET MONSTER

When I saw the day so bright,
I didn't think I'd get a fright,
But when I saw the monster come,
I knew I wouldn't have any fun.

When I went to the loo I saw,
The monster eating the toilet door!
His tummy was extremely fat,
But he'd just eaten the toilet rats!

My mum said 'Yey,'
My dad said 'Wahey,'
And of course he's stayed
With us all day!

Susanna Hamlyn (10)
Sherborne House School

IT'S DARK IN THE CORNER

It's dark in the corner,
Oh, it's very scary,
Is there anything there that's hairy?
Maybe it's got lots of legs,
Or perhaps six hundred eyes,
It's going to lay a million eggs,
And then . . . oh God . . . think of it multiplied!
Is it big, green and lumpy?
I'm getting closer now, I feel very jumpy,
Agghhhh! It's on me, help!
Even the dog yelped!
Oww! It's sharp, it's a goat.
No, you dope it's a hairy coat!

Elouise Godwin (11)
Sherborne House School

GROWN-UPS

Grown-ups get to stay up late
why can't we, for goodness sake?

I sneak downstairs and watch some TV
I watch Rugrats on BBC.

I go to the kitchen and take every single sweet,
and have a midnight feast with lots of things to eat.

Then I go back to my comfy bed
I put my soft pillow back over my head.

But after all I don't know why grown-ups just can't say yes,
but sometimes they're nice, I must confess.

Matthew Oliver (8)
Sherborne House School

HOME SWEET HOME

There's no place like home,
It's better than the Dome.
Why do I leave,
And try to succeed.
A zoo trip that's boring,
Watching animals snoring.
A museum with signs saying 'Don't touch!'
A cold sausage for lunch.
Oh I wish I could stay
At the place where I play
I think I'll just moan
And they might take me home.

Richard de Vere (11)
Sherborne House School

DREAMS

I snuggled in my bed that night,
With my eyes closed tight,
I thought I was going on holiday
In the middle of sunny May.
All of a sudden in my head
I noticed that I wasn't snuggled up in my bed,
I am now walking in a cave that is dark, dark, dark.
From the cave I hear a growling bark,
I see a monster crunching bones crunch, crunch, crunch.
You look nice for lunch!
The monster was chasing me faster and faster, behind me,
Oh no! I've tripped up on my knee
I wriggled about in my bed,
But the nightmare is in my head.
The dream has gone far enough
I think it is time to wake up.

Amandeep Dhillon (9)
Sherborne House School

MILLENNIUM

M illions of people gather for this day
I   t gets darker as the New Year draws nearer
L   asers light the sky with many colours
L   oud bangs of fireworks fill my ears
E   verlasting, I hope this day will be
N ow voices are cheering along
N o one will be asleep for this New Year
I   ncredible lights are an amazing sight
U ntil someone shouts . . .
M illennium is here, Happy New Year.

Lucy Oliver (11)
Sherborne House School

No, But

Have you learnt your tables?
No . . .
But I thought of my chairs!

Did you have a wash last night?
No . . .
But I thought of my chairs!

Have you done your homework?
No . . .
But neither did Bart Simpson!

Did you watch the history video?
No . . .
But Kate Winslet was great!

Have you cleaned the car?
No . . .
But the birds think it's okay!

Did you eat your lunch?
No . . .
But the pigs liked it!

Okay, so let's start again,
And no . . . No buts this time,

Yes, but . . .

Emma Bowyer (11)
Sherborne House School

WRITE A POEM

My thoughts won't come
This isn't much fun
How do you write a poem?

I've worked hard all day
I just want to play
How do you write a poem?

I called my mum
She was too busy to come
How do you write a poem?

I yelled at my sister
What a nuisance I missed her
How do you write a poem?

So I woofed at the dog
But he went for a jog
How do you write a poem?

Then I sat in the bath
And had a good laugh
How do you write a poem?

I put my pen to paper
And not much later
Yippee, I'd written my poem!

Francesca Ackroyd (9)
Sherborne House School

TROLL FRIENDS

Trolls are fat, trolls are ugly,
Trolls are very smelly too,
Their sickly smiles, big horrible noses,

My troll has pink hair and the other has orange,
Hair so frizzy it makes you dizzy,
I think they're special because they're mine
We get along just fine.

I love my trolls and they love me,
I can talk to them anytime,
They listen to my secrets and never tell a soul,
They're real to me and mine forever.

Anna Janakiraman (9)
Sherborne House School

CHRISTMAS DAY

On Christmas Day
The snow's great fun
You throw snowballs at everyone.

Jesus was born on the 25th
Celebrate the birth and every gift.

You get toy guns, and plastic thumbs,
You eat too much turkey and stuffing too,
The crackers go bang and so do you.
Carols are sung around the world,
It's a happy time for all concerned.

Oliver Cox (9)
Sherborne House School

THE MAGICAL DREAM

The Olympics . . . 2004
I'm sitting in a boat
Holding an oar!

The starter says 'Go!'
The race is on
The Italians are leading

Somebody caught a crab
The Italians!
We take the lead!

50 metres to go
The Spanish are catching up
I keep on going and going
And going and going

And then the hooter blasts . . .

Jonathan Higginson (10)
Sherborne House School

WAR

War is very bad
If I was in one, I'd be sad.
There are lots of people getting bombed and killed
If I saw that, I wouldn't be thrilled.
Army doctors help the injured troops
Whilst armoured men float down on parachutes.
There are children being sent to far away places
Hoping to see all of their family's faces.
Rationing made it hard to eat
Especially when you fancied something sweet.

Simon de Villiers (8)
Sherborne House School

MONSTERS IN THE DARK

When I woke up one stormy night,
I saw a thing that gave me a fright.
It stood there quite still
For hours until
I fell asleep,
By counting sheep.

I dreamed of a monster
That looked like a lobster
With four foot long pincers
With the power of mincers.

It waggled its claws
And then showed its paws.
Which were big brown and hairy
And looked very scary.

I called for my mum
Who said 'Don't be dumb
the monster's not bad
It's only your dad!'

Emily Howe (8)
Sherborne House School

UNDER MY BED

Under my bed
Where nobody goes
There's five fat monsters
With bright orange toes
Roger, Toby, Frederick, Dan
And a baby with spots
They call him Stan

Charles Fenton (10)
Sherborne House School

WISPA

I have a cat called Wispa
She is grey and white
She stays out in the daytime
And sleeps with me at night
She hides in our wheelbarrow
And plays with another cat
His name is Casper
He is grey, fluffy and fat!
Wispa is such fun to watch
She runs and chases her tail
But she always stops for her dinner
At five o'clock without fail.

Olivia Clarke (8)
Sherborne House School

BILLS

Bills boring bills
Bills boring bills
Bills big bills
Bills small bills
Bills for boys
Bills for toys
Bills for girls
Bills for wine
Bills for turpentine
Bills for the phone
Bills for the gas
Bills please *Stop!*

Rory Yonge (8)
Sherborne House School

UNICORNS

In the middle of our forest
One dark night
I heard the crackling of twigs,
And saw white flashes of light.

I thought it was a pony
But as I got nearer
Its silver horn glittered,
As the moon shone clearer.

I got closer still
And said 'Don't be afraid'
As it walked slowly towards me
And good friends we made.

I gave it a pat on the neck
And then stroked its head.
I jumped on its back
And 'Let's go!' I said.

It jumped over a log
And we started to fly
What an adventure
As we flew through the sky.

Remy Ellis (8)
Sherborne House School

THE DAY I PLAYED FOR SAINTS

Woke up, got dressed
Had some food
A letter with my name
It said 'Sam Nugent
You've been picked
To play in today's big game.'

'Yippee!' I said
'I'll definitely go
I'll get my kit right now
My football boots are shiny clean
And everyone will say wow!'

Sam Nugent (9)
Sherborne House School

DIDN'T BELIEVE HIM

This boy, Thomas Williams
He said that his family are millionaires.
I didn't believe him.

There's another boy called Derek Drew
It looks just like he'd been flushed down the loo,
He said he had
But I didn't believe him.

The boy who lives just down the road from me,
Said he'd been in an aeroplane, you see
But I said I didn't believe him.

There's this other boy
Who said he'd got such a brilliant toy
I didn't believe him!

I don't like this boy called Samuel Sam,
He said he'd been in his sister's pram,
I said I didn't believe him.

But this is true,
I flew to Mars,
I circled the stars.
Honest!
Don't you believe me?

Georgia Howard (9)
Sherborne House School

THE MONSTER'S TOILET

The monster's toilet
All smelly and gooey

There's slime all over the sink
And it's slippery on the floor

The loo is large enough
To fit a dinosaur

His toilet roll is dirty
His toilet seat is sick

And when it gets too dirty
He'll just give it a lick!

Josh Healy (11)
Sherborne House School

DICK'S WARNING

On Christmas Day I thought it was May
There once was a boy called Dick.
I once yelled 'Come on Dick!
Give me a lick! Of that fabulous ice cream you've got.'
'Not for you rotter!
You idiot clotter!
This ice cream is for my sis!
I'll toast you alive
I might roast you alive,
If you lay one finger on this!'

Christopher McPhie (8)
Sherborne House School

FANTASTIC FOOD

Food is fantastic, except when it's fish
To tell you the truth, it's my very worst dish
Now give me pizza, a burger or chips
And I'll coat them in ketchup, licking my lips.

Gingerbread men, with smarties for buttons
Are great enough to join the gluttons
But treacle tart with lumpy custard
Is worse than the hottest English mustard!

School potatoes, all black inside
Are bad enough to make me hide
But give me Marks and Spencer's mash
And to the table I will dash.

Sweets and chocolate are wonderful things
While munching on these, my little heart sings
There is only one problem, what could that be?
The dentist of course, no sugar for me!

Olivia Warner (9)
Sherborne House School

FLYING

I wish I could fly
Up there in the sky.
I would fly like a bird
Although it sounds absurd.
If this wish came true
I would fly up there in the blue.

Zoe Fairhurst (8)
Sherborne House School

THE GHOST TRAIN

The ghost train goes very fast
It smells and yells and has steam like fluff
Nobody can see the ghost train.

It winds along and goes bang through the doors
Skeletons jump out, and give you a fright.
Nobody can see the ghost train.

Have I really been on board?
Shall I do it again tonight?
Nobody can see the ghost train.

Thomas Ross (9)
Sherborne House School

ALIENS

Aliens are always here
They are very, very near,
Crawling closer in a line
Going forwards into time
Creeping into all your beds
Then they get inside your head
Going up into your brain
(This might cause a little pain)
Aliens are always here
They are very, very near

Sophie Jones (9)
Sherborne House School

IN THE FUTURE

In the future
Aliens will rule the Earth,
Nothing there, not a single birth,
Aliens are cruel, they will destroy everything.

In the future
Men will live behind bars,
They will only ever dream of seeing
The sun and stars.

In the future
Animals will die,
They will float up to the sky
It will be bad, it will be sad.

In the future,
Families will still love each other.
Sometimes love will drift away
But it will return as soon as we say
In the future!

Natasha Lijka (8)
Sherborne House School

THERE'S A MONSTER UNDER MY BED

Mum, mum,
There's a monster under my bed!
His eyes are glaring red.
Will he eat me?
Will he squeeze me?
He's green and gooey and grabs my leg.
Oh no! Now he's *in* my bed.
Whoops! It's just Fred, my ted!

Theo Pack (10)
Sherborne House School

CHOCOLATE WORLD

Chocolate World is full of food
Where everyone is in a good mood.

Chocolate World is full of fun
But mind it doesn't melt in the sun!

Chocolate World is full of chocolate people
With a chocolate church and chocolate steeple.

Chocolate World is huge and round
Where chocolate animals can be found.

But most of all Chocolate World is yummy
When I smell it, there's a rumble in my tummy.

Rebecca Allsop (9)
Sherborne House School

THERE'S A MONSTER LIVING UNDER THE SINK!

There's a monster
living under the sink.
It's red and white,
black and pink.
What do I do,
now that he's there?
Do I shoot to kill him
or rip off his hair?
It is not fair
that he is still there.
The monster that lives
under the sink.

Anna-Marie Broadway (9)
Sherborne House School

THE WITCH'S RECIPE

Wings of birds that never occurred
A tiger's tie
That I thought
That would do for a pie!

A fin of a fish
That was put on a dish
A dead man's finger
Made of ginger

But she had made
Bird's Eye Fish Fingers!

Mary-Anne Trant (10)
Sherborne House School

FIREWORKS

Fireworks go bang!
In the middle of the night.
They sizzle and swizzle
And give you a fright.
They twirl and glow
Like a thousand candles in the night.

They're bright and fantastic
And light up the sky.
But after a while
They eventually die.

Simon Young (10)
Sherborne House School

SUMMER

Summer, summer
We're in the pool
Summer, summer
It's really cool

Summer, summer
We're having fun
Summer, summer
For everyone

Summer, summer
Flowers and trees
Summer, summer
Birds and bees

Summer, summer
Holidays
Summer, summer
Lazy days

Summer, summer
Sand and sea
Summer, summer
Treats for tea

Summer, summer
Best time of year
Summer, summer
Now it's here!

Chelsey Cooper (9)
Sherborne House School

WHY YOU SHOULDN'T BE A BABY-SITTER

Could you get your clothes on for school,
Please!
Why?
Because you need to wear a uniform.
Why?
Because you'll freeze with nothing on.
Why?
I don't know.
Why?
Because I'm not clever enough.
Why?
Because God didn't create me properly,
He forgot my brain
Why?
Because whoever created Him
Forgot His brain too!
Why?
Get your clothes on!
Why?
I've been through this already.
Why?
Will you stop saying why!
What?
Stop picking on me!
I'm only the babysitter!
Why?

Scarlett Cox (10)
Sherborne House School

THE MONSTER

In the dark of the room
I hear a sound
Is it a monster?
Green and hairy
Big and scary?
I'm not sure
I sit very still
I listen and wait
No, it's not
It's only my mate.

Emma Stanswood (10)
Sherborne House School

ANIMALS

An ant is as small as dust
An elephant is as big as a house
A bird can fly like a plane
A rat is as dirty as mud.

A parrot squawks like a monkey
A cat is as comfy as a cushion.
A frog is as green as grass
A bee is as noisy as a buzzer.

A spider is as black as a blackboard
A fish is as colourful as the rainbow,
A sheep is as fluffy as a cloud
A tortoise is as slow as a slug.

Timira Patel (8)
Upham CE Primary School

PET POEM

Cats, furry and fluffy,
Dogs, hairy and scruffy.
Please let me have one.
Mum says 'No, no, *no*!'

Horses, good at running
Pot-bellied pigs very cunning.
Please let me have one.
Mum says 'No, no, *no*!'

Mice, terribly wiggly,
Monkeys, very giggly.
Please let me have one,
Mum says 'No, no, *no!*'

Spiders, very creepy
Guinea pigs, very weepy.
Please let me have one.
Mum says 'No, no, *no!*'

Ducks very flappy
Woodpeckers very tappy.
Please let me have one,
Mum says 'No, no, *no!*'

Giraffes very tall
Ants very small.
Please let me have one.
Mum says 'No, no, *no!*'

Fish horrid and slimy,
Rabbits terribly whiny.
Please don't get one.
Mum says 'Yes, yes, yes!'

Abbie Butler (8)
Upham CE Primary School

THE RAINFOREST

The rainforest
You never know what's gonna happen
You might see hissing slithering snakes
You might see roaring tigers
You might see creepy-crawly spiders
The shimmering, shining sun
Gleams through the trees.
Cheeky monkeys jumping from the trees.

Alice Lowe (8)
Upham CE Primary School

AMAZING ANIMALS

Monkeys munching on marshmallows
Elephants eating
Sharp tigers' teeth tugging on rope
Rhinos racing
Lions roaring
Snakes slithering in sacks
Giraffes standing as still as statues
Kangaroos jumping like jumping jellybeans
Eagles flying like rockets
Lizards running at the speed of light.

James Chamberlain (8)
Upham CE Primary School

THE SHIMMERING SUN

The sun is glistening in the sky,
It's shining bright, way up high,
All the children come out to play
On this lovely summer's day.

Poppies dancing in the breeze,
As the sunlight peeps through the trees.
This lovely weather is such a delight
It makes me feel happy and bright.

Alice Miles (9)
Upham CE Primary School

PONIES

Ponies jumping around
Over wooden stiles and the muddy ground.
Chocolate brown
Golden as the sun
All different kinds.
Mane as fluffy as a cloud
Legs galloping rapidly
Like a clumsy clown.
Body as cuddly as a teddy
A soft velvet nose.

Jenna Counsell (9)
Upham CE Primary School

MY HAMSTER

Sleeps in the day like a Vampire
Is as furry as a bunny.
Has teeth as yellow as the sun
Fur as black as the darkest night.
As cute as a cuddly bear
Enormous black eyes like coal
But most of all he loves me.

William Peters (8)
Upham CE Primary School

CATS

I love cats they are my best friends,
Sooty and Sweep are their names.
They're up to mischief, playing their games,
They get along together and they scratch the beds.
Mum rattles their dishes
They'll have to be fed
They'll look and they'll hunt until it's time for bed.
There's nothing more loving than hearing them purr
When I cuddle and kiss them and tickle
Their fur.

Katie Spencer (8)
Upham CE Primary School

THE MOON

The moon is magical
It's pale and white,
It shimmers in the darkness
And lights up the night.

It runs across the sky
Trying to catch the sun,
But is always on its own
When the day is done.

Lydia Skene (8)
Upham CE Primary School

GOD'S GARDEN

My garden's full of peaceful flowers
They grow from day to day
Their colours are so beautiful
In every perfect way.

The daffodils are yellow
The bluebells just like ink
Their smell is so lovely
A gift from me to you.

Simon Romsey (8)
Upham CE Primary School

DOLPHINS IN THE DEEP

Dolphins are intelligent, brainy and smart
They're as clever as you and I.
Dolphins are beautiful, lovely and cute.
Dolphins are as graceful as a ballerina
Their skin is smoother than the smoothest silk.
People say a dolphin's skin is slimy, but it isn't!
But sometimes a shark comes along and *chomp!*

Jasmin Knox-Langford (8)
Upham CE Primary School

THE FLOOD

It was pouring down outside
It was gurgling in the street,
It was tumbling through the ditches
And heading for our house.

The trees were down
The electricity was off
The fences were flat
Hooray!
No school today!

Georgina Stott (8)
Upham CE Primary School

WHY ME?

Why is it me who gets picked on?
I didn't do anything wrong.
All I ask is to join in with them,
Join in playing along.
Inside I feel scared and worried
Lonely like one cloud in the sky.
It's only my first day at school
And I've already got tears in my eyes.
Nobody here really likes me
It's like I don't even exist.
People can be mean and cruel
I wish I could tell them this.

Emily Goddard (9)
Upham CE Primary School

MY HORSES

My horses are brown
black and white.
With beautiful long manes.
The black one is like the
deepest, darkest night.
My white one is like
a fluffy white cloud.
My brown one is chocolate.
Their tack is sparkling.
When I ride them
They're my horses.

Sophie Hammond (8)
Upham CE Primary School

SPACE

If there ever was a really great place
I'm sure it must be outer space,
And why do I think space is cool?
Because there is no flipping school!

I wonder what it's really like
Away up there in space?
Is there life on Mars perhaps
Or another living race?
I wonder if it's dark or light
Or simply has just day and night?
I wonder if it's cold or hot
Or whether there are plants or not?
I wish I was a spaceman so that I could
Touch the stars
I'd float across the galaxy
I'd walk upon the moon
And maybe I'd find the answers to the
Mysteries of space!
But maybe I would disappear,
Gone without a trace!
Joe kidnapped by aliens whilst visiting
Outer Space!

Joseph Seward (9)
Wallisdean Junior School

POLLUTION

You construct the countryside
But you let us destroy it.
Why can't you make us
Destroy houses and build flats?
That will use space well.

Why can't you tell them to put
It in the bin?
Empty it every day, it smells
Bad, recycle it.

You let them dump it in
The ground, you let us burn
It up now, you let us build
Pyramids from rubbish, it ruins
The countryside it's *unfair.*

You let the water destroy
Houses in February 2000 (Mozambique)
Drought in May 2000 (India)
Where is it going to strike next?

You let us start wars, I can't
Bare you to let us. If we
Start World War III we
I mean, we might die out.

Nicholas Pugh (10)
Westbourne Primary School

EAGLE

Ferocious
savage
wild
protective

Cunning
swift
the lord of the
skies.
The eagle.

Sam Long (10)
Westbourne Primary School

ANTELOPE

Antelope running
Danger coming, coming to chase
and take away.
Try and run, tiger coming
closer to catch its prey
I just want to say
go for something else, go away.
He follows me all
the way to my den.
I kick them out
and shout
'Get out!'
They run away
and say
'You'll pay.'
We eat in the field peacefully
without
a sound . . .
Wait a minute!
What's that sound?
Oh no!
It's them!

Kelsey Collins (10)
Westbourne Primary School

ANIMAL'S PLEA

You are unfair, hurtful,
You do not understand,
How much you hurt me
I am pleading, set me free.

You destroy my friends, family and home,
You are careless, unkind,
You are almost destroying me
My life is in tatters.

You think you can rule me,
But you can't
You show no mercy,
Killing is your growing hobby.

You are not thinking of the damage you do,
Look now, what I am
You have lots, I have nothing.
I am me, you are you.

I cannot be you
For I am I,
And that will not change,
As long as you are you
And I am me.

David Burtonwood (11)
Westbourne Primary School

BE FRIENDS

Love for you,
Is not true,
We won't be friends, won't be friends,
Let us not be as one,
We won't be friends, won't be friends.

Live no more,
And play wars,
Don't spread love people, don't love.

There's no race,
No race now,
Don't need safety, don't need safety,
Let's make war and hate each other,
Don't need safety, don't be safe.

Don't get me wrong,
My love is strong,
Be kind to each other, be kind to each other,
Let's live as one for ever,
Be kind to each other, be kind,
So let this land be
Ours,
Ours
And
Ours,
So be as one, as one in mind.

Eleanor Pearson (9)
Westbourne Primary School

LIVE FOR EVER

The ankle high creatures that come crawling to your feet,
The spirits you see, seem never to live.
You just live for eternity.
You'll last for ever, but not me.

The tallest creatures that you've ever seen,
Still come walking to see you sleep,
My soul in me will never die,
But will live with you, my friend.

The time is coming
I'm getting weaker
I fear I will not go with you.
For the sin that has forsaken me and my world,
Soon I will live in eternity with you my friend
Soon I will be with you again!

Bethany Hardingham ((11)
Westbourne Primary School

THE WOLF

The wolf needs a pack
He can run fast to catch his prey in the summer.
He wants his family
He is wild, like a bear
The wolf needs warm-blooded food.
He runs like a cheater.
He splashes like a baby in a stream
He howls like an owl
The wolf needs a loving mother.

Aaron Watts (10)
Westbourne Primary School

WILD THINGS

Trumpeting
blowing
shouting with its trunk.
Rampaging
crazily,
stomping its feet.
Flipping,
flapping
flopping its ears.
The biggest mammal in Africa,
Grey
thick skin
loud consumer.
It's an elephant!

Oliver Rea (10)
Westbourne Primary School

BUSHBABY

Not eternal
Mammal
Clutches, clasps
With delicate grip
Bushbaby
Creature of the night
Vast, bright eyes
To capture moths
Nightly hunter
Tender, touch.
Baby of the bush.

Jay J Norbury (11)
Westbourne Primary School

PLUTO

Pluto, place with no
Life
Uninhabitable
Too cold
In our solar system
Pluto is last place you want to be
Cold, misty, freezing blue
Cold as an ice cube
Waiting in the freezer for you
Far away as far as can be
A billion miles away
Small as a tennis ball
When it's winter it's even colder
Whilst snow is falling
Since Pluto is far, step one foot and you die
Wherever Pluto is it is still small
Whenever you go you will never come back
As it is so, so cold
It is never hot.

Laura Gladman (8)
Westbourne Primary School

THE CHEETAH

The cheetah speeds through the forest
darting faster and faster
He hides under tree trunks
Watching all around
He crawls on his tummy;
His sharp claws digging into the ground
Then - pounce! The prey is his.

Liam Scutt (10)
Westbourne Primary School

SPACESHIPS

Spaceships are
big
Spaceships are
small
they can be
all *sizes.*

Dangerously *big*
dangerously *small.*
Cool
We have lift-off!
Millions . . .
of miles . . .
from home.
Mission accomplished.

Eddie Johnson (8)
Westbourne Primary School

SNAKES

I hiss like the wind
You might think I am a cat.
I appear when not expected,
I never lose a hiding game.
I look like an 's' shaped letter
As I look for prey.
I am ready and alert
All small I am
I am very vicious
Watch out! I might be about!

Emma Veltom (9)
Westbourne Primary School

TOUCAN

Soars though the air like a comet on its round,
Lands like an aeroplane on wheels.
As busy as a goldmine doing its daily work,
Eats food like a whirlwind sucking up houses and cars.
Its beak like an overgrown banana with black marks.
Flies through miles of skies, brightening up the land,
It's always on the lookout for somewhere to land.

Derren Limbert (10)
Westbourne Primary School

PLUTO

Pluto, frozen planet
Makes an infinite snow arc
Like a snowball in the night sky.
Remote
Unemotional,
Cold, silver and white.
Moves through a frozen patch of stars.
A frozen sea.

William Hurst (9)
Westbourne Primary School

THE MOON

The moon shimmering in rivers and lakes,
Like a lighthouse afloat in the sky.
Floating like a lonely glider flying across the night.
The sky is painted silver
Moon shining in the highest sky.
Our guide at night.

Justin Clark (10)
Westbourne Primary School

OUR PLANET

A peaceful planet
The Earth
Like a green and blue mass
The Earth.

The trees with green life
The forest.
The water with blue life
The sea.
The sand with yellow life
The desert.

The human's black polluted cities
The disaster!

Mike Goodbourn (10)
Westbourne Primary School

WAR

We fought for our land
Our land we fought for
Guns caused death
And death caused despair.

Our country fought day and night
Day and night our country fought.
They fought for their lives
Their lives they fought for.

They protected God's country
God's country they protected.
They saved God's country
A land that was free.

Jo-Jo Hamer-Philip (8)
Westbourne Primary School

POLLUTION

I am not you
but you will not
give me a chance,
will not let me be me

If I were you
but you know
I am not you
but you will not
let me be me

You meddle, interfere
with my waters
as if they were yours
as if you were me

You are unfair, unwise
foolish to think
that I can be you
talk, act
and be wasteful like you

God made me me
He made you you
For God's sake
don't pollute me!

David Evans (11)
Westbourne Primary School

UNFAIR

I am not you
You are rich
and I am poor
you won't let me be me

You work for money
but I stand here begging
I am dressed in rags
sleeping in old bags
but you, smartly dressed, sleep in a duvet

You are warm
I am cold
you don't need help
I do need help

You have toys
I don't have anything
You're healthy
I'm skinny
Not like you

You have family
I don't, I'm lonely
You don't know my feelings
You're glad you're not me.

Fiona Hamer-Philip (10)
Westbourne Primary School

RHINO

Powerful protector
Unskilful gymnast
Hulking charger
Rhino . . .

Runs like a tank
Bulletproof armour
Granite horn
Rhino . . .

Rock hard giant
Muscular defender
Sensitive consumer
Rhino . . .

Carl Stevenson (11)
Westbourne Primary School

WITCH'S BREW

Toe of lizard, tongue of frog,
head of rat and howl of dog,
Cluck of chicken, screech of bat,
eye of weasel, paw of cat.
Mix it up and stir it well,
to make a magic monster spell.
Leech's brain, thinly chopped,
pus of pimple, freshly popped.
Leg of spider, throat of toad,
squish of hedgehog pulled off a road.
Mix it up and stir it well,
to make a magic monster spell.

Barry Ronald (10)
Wildground Junior School

MY BIKE

I have a bike like a racing winner,
Racing down a gigantic hill.

Tossing and turning racing down,
Then I fell straight to the ground.

I have a bike like a racing winner,
Racing down a gigantic hill.

Then I scream so loud, so loud,
There is blood gushing to the ground.

I have a bike like a racing winner,
Racing down a gigantic hill.

Then Mum says 'Oh daughter of mine,
Don't you worry, you'll soon be fine.'

I have a bike like a racing winner,
Racing down a gigantic hill.

Then I look into the mirror,
Oh my dear I can't see any clearer.

I have a bike like a racing winner,
Racing down a gigantic hill.

Two weeks later and not a scar in sight,
And I'm back on my racing bike.

I have a bike like a racing winner,
Racing down a gigantic hill.

Helen Canning (10)
Wildground Junior School

SADNESS GROWING

Heart beating
Pulse pumping
Tears tickling
Anger growing
Fear opened
Mind coiled
House ruined
Broken hearted
Sadness erupted.

Melissa Franklin (10)
Wildground Junior School

ANGRY

Heart thumping,
Pulse racing,
Muscles tense,
Fists clenched,
Sadness rising,
Tele shouting,
Blood rushing,
Brain pounding,
Overload,
Body . . . *explodes!*

Iain Powell (10)
Wildground Junior School

NATURE

One oddly oblong octopus,
Two tough talking turtles,
Three thoughtful thinking thrushes,
Four friendly flowery fish,
Five flapping funny finches,
Six sulking swimming swordfish,
Seven silly sour snails,
Eight enormous irritating elephants,
Nine nipping nosy nightingales.
Ten teasing tabby cats.

Stephanie Randell (8)
Wildground Junior School

MY DAD

My dad has been acting strange
Like walking around in chains
He sleeps in the day
He wakes in the night
Then disappears out of sight.

He sleeps in a long black coffin
With gold around the rim
I'm getting the wrong idea about him.

Charlotte Ferris (11)
Wildground Junior School

I Am A Brownie

I am a Brownie
I like it very much
We meet on Thursday evenings
To laugh and play.
We journey on our pathways
Learning as we go
To be a better Brownie
Wherever we may go.

Lauren Stubbington (7)
Wildground Junior School

My Rabbits

I love my rabbits,
they're really cute,
they look so sweet,
when I come to give them a treat.

Andrew Canning (8)
Wildground Junior School

The Dragon

The fierce beast lies
waiting,
A giant lizard
waiting,
terrible, fire-breathing
waiting,
waiting for a friend in his loneliness.

Alison Kenworthy (10)
Wildground Junior School

MOTOR BIKE RACING TRACK

Motor bikes racing, smashing, bashing, jumping,
breaking metal in the gravel.
People cheering, shouting, clapping,
screaming in the crowd.
Motor bikes cracking, sliding, skidding, on the track,
Motor bikes in the pits, ready to go,
motor bikes out of the pits.
People cheering as the winner goes by.

Ashley Squires (9)
Whiteley Primary School

PARADISE

The sky as blue as a whale,
A lady as beautiful as a pink petal,
Her hair as ripply as waves,
Her dress as white as snow,
Her scarf swaying in the breeze.

Luke Clifford (9)
Whiteley Primary School

ME AND CHOCOLATE

I can't live without chocolate
I must have three tons a day
Do not take my chocolate away
Or you know what I'll do
And you'll pay the price.
You'll be sitting there eating rice!

Thomas Roostan (10)
Whiteley Primary School

THE HALLOWE'EN NIGHT

It was Hallowe'en, all was quiet
On the 31st of October 1668
When
The oldest house of the street lit up
And the door came open.
In the doorway there stood a shadow
Holding what appeared to be a broomstick
The pilgrims all came with torches of fire
When
The Royal Highness said
'Let it be hung'
And so the mysterious figure was never seen again!

Emily Brogan (10)
Whiteley Primary School

THE LAKE

The water as gentle as falling snow,
The bridge as still as a tree branch,
The trees as beautiful as the sunset,
The plants as wonderful as a Monet painting,
The shadows as small as mice,
The leaves as dangly as falling feathers,
The night as calm as a ballerina,
The waterfall as pretty as flowers,
The stones as sparkly as glitter,
The lily pads floating like little green boats,
The grass like a bird flying through the sky,
The flowers as light as the sky.

Catherine De Roure (8)
Whiteley Primary School

MESSY JESSÉ

There was a girl whose name was Jessé,
And she was really very messy
She never ever tidied her room
She ate chocolate mousse without a spoon
Her mum was sick, her dad was tired
Her sister picked up a gun and fired
The bullet was meant to hit Jess's back
Instead it hit the family cat
The cat was crying, her mum was cross
Then Dad shouted, 'I am the boss'
Jessie was screaming, her sister was mad
And her parents weren't very glad
And that just about covers the family
The cat was a really very big tragedy.

Jessé Taylor (9)
Whiteley Primary School

WINTER

The wall as red as fire,
The snow as white as sheep,
The girl is as thoughtful as an artist,
The sky as blue as water,
The trees as black as coal,
The robin is as beautiful as a butterfly,
The hat as bright as the sun,
Her hair as brown as bark,
It is as cold as ice,
Her cheeks as red as rosy apples.

Emma Shear (9)
Whiteley Primary School

MY CATS

My cats are ragdoll cats,
they hang around most of the day
that's why they're called ragdoll cats.

Daisy loves feet, we don't know why
She licks my mum's tights,
hopefully she doesn't mean to, but she might.

Merlin's coat is messy and thick,
his coat is darker than cream,
he sits around all day and dreams.

Merlin is not as bad as Daisy,
they're my two troublesome cats,
but remember they're only kittens!

Erin Miller (10)
Whiteley Primary School

VALENTINE'S DAY

V   alentine's Day
A   dmirer
L   ove
E   verywhere
N   ew
T   ime
I   mportant
N   ow
E   njoy
S   pecial.

Christina Taliadoros (10)
Whiteley Primary School

MY CLASS (5W)

Emma is working really hard,
I'm making a secret card,
Dominic is concentrating and chewing his pencil,
Whilst Jess is doing some special stencils,
Sam is giggling with Seb as he does,
Amy is always making a fuss!
Dinner lady comes in,
As Miss White is throwing her pen in the bin,
Ashley is drawing sails,
And Adam is biting his nails,
Erin is reading her books,
Christina is showing off her looks,
At the end of lunch,
We sit down and wait.

Phillipa Brown (9)
Whiteley Primary School

IMAGINE

Imagine a nose
As big as a hose.
Imagine a bear
As hairy as my hair.
Imagine a glass
As big as a class.
Imagine an eye
As big as a spy.
Imagine me
As small as a flea . . .

Oliver James (9)
Whiteley Primary School

SUPPLY TEACHERS

When your teacher isn't at school,
you always have to act very cool,
We had a teacher called Mrs Bloom one day,
and this is how it went . . .

We started in the morning, bright and early,
We saw her hair was brown and curly.
We sat down and started chatting,
she joined in.

After assembly we started maths,
She didn't scratch her hair like she had gnats.
After maths we played a game,
And talked about it at play.

At 11.00 we had literacy,
It got so hot she wondered if there was any AC.
At lunchtime we talked again,
about no one but her.

After lunch we had ICT and art,
For lunch she said she had a jam tart.
At last it was the end of the day,
For the first time I didn't say 'Hooray!'

Amy Achwal (9)
Whiteley Primary School

WALKING THROUGH A JUNGLE

I am walking through the jungle
Treading on the leaves,
Listening to the birds sing,
Watching monkeys in the trees.

Snakes that slither, shift between,
Branches full of evergreen.
Warm and humid is the air,
Sticky is my face and hair.

Hear the rushing of a waterfall,
As it tumbles over rocks,
A place to rest and now feel cool.
And time to dry my socks!

Hear the orang-utang swinging in the air,
Swinging in the monkey hair
Eating flies all day long,
Eating them when he's going along.

The elephant is walking on tiptoes,
Quietly sneaking wherever she goes.
The baby is crying
It makes a very big noise.

Hollie James (9)
Whiteley Primary School

THE STORM

He sends down the snowstorm
With anger and strength
No one can stop him
But run and hide.

Screaming and shouting
The blizzard's about
He stamps his feet
And blows the wind out.

He reaches out with his finger of ice
And touches you twice
You shiver and shudder
And cling to each other.

He stops and looks and smiles at the view
The children come out but only a few
He watches them as they laugh and play
He goes now but he'll be back another day.

Samantha Jordan (10)
Whiteley Primary School

MY ROOM

My room is my room,
with light purple walls,
My room is my room,
with bunk beds standing tall.

My room is my room,
with CDs everywhere,
My room is my room,
with beanies on a chair.

My room is my room,
with a poster on my door,
My room is my room,
with lots and lots more.

My room is my room,
and there's nothing you can change,
My room is my room,
and it will always be the same.

Chloé Brunsdon (9)
Whiteley Primary School

A WALK IN THE PARK

I'm walking in the park
on a sunny day,
It's making all my thoughts
just fly away,
The butterfly is making a gentle breeze,
The pollen on the plants
makes me want to sneeze.

The children on the swings
start to scream and shout,
Like the kids over there
on the roundabout,
As the dog chases the ducks
on the lake,
He's called by his walker,
'Come here, Jake, *Jake!'*
The songbirds sing
a cheerful song,
Look at that crane,
his neck is so long,
There are children
over there on a slide,
There are children over there
who try to hide.

My bed at home
is waiting for me,
I'll be in my bed
just after tea,
Now the wonders of the park
have been said,
Now I'm going home
to go to bed.

Kate Beattie (8)
Whiteley Primary School

WHAT IS . . . THE WORLD?

The world is a big blue ball
floating in the air.

The world is a spinning top
twirling and spinning around and around.

It is an old football
being mis-used again and again.

It is a soft apple
being cut into pieces.

It is a blue and green ink splodge
that has faded throughout the years!

Charlotte Hill (10)
Whiteley Primary School

A DAY IN MY CLASS

Sam's got very nimble fingers,
At playtime David never lingers.
Here's me with my hand high up in the air,
While Rikki's daydreaming without a care.
Katie Marsh is out with Mrs Latter,
In the cloakroom there's a bang and a clatter.
Jack Stanton, he is Mars Bar crazy,
My buddy, Yasmine, is as sweet as a daisy.
Nicole with her lovely golden locks,
Poor Daniel, he's got chicken pox.
Here comes Laura, my best friend,
Sorry my poem must come to an end.

Katie Smith (10)
Whiteley Primary School